LOS ANGELES IN CIVIL WAR DAYS

LOS ANGELES IN CIVIL WAR DAYS 1860–1865

JOHN W. ROBINSON

UNIVERSITY OF OKLAHOMA PRESS : NORMAN

Library of Congress Cataloging-in-Publication Data
Robinson, John W., 1929–
Los Angeles in Civil War days, 1860–1865 / by John W. Robinson.
173 p., ill. ; 25 cm.
Includes bibliographical references and index
ISBN 978-0-8061-4312-5 (alk. paper
1. Los Angeles (Calif.)—History—Civil War, 1861–1865.

F869.L857 R63
979.4/94/04

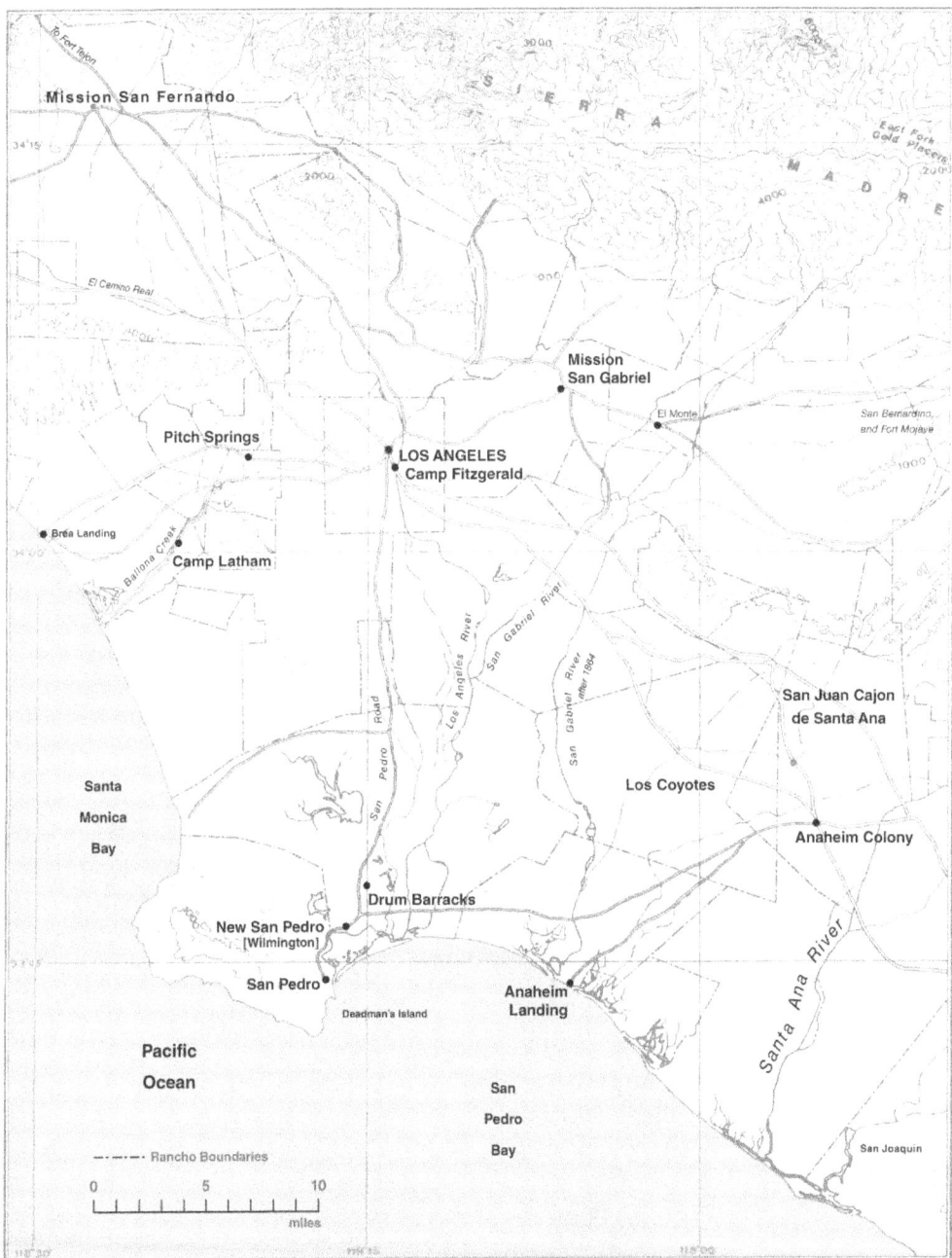

Los Angeles and vicinity, circa 1860. Based on a map by Laurence G. Jones, whose sources included topographic maps of the U.S. Geological Survey and Army Map Service, 1899–1968, and George W. Kirkman, *Kirkman-Harriman Pictorial and Historical Map of Los Angeles County* (1937).

PREFACE

The American Civil War is certainly one of the best documented conflicts in history. Few struggles anywhere, anytime, can equal it in the sheer volume of literary coverage. For more than a century, an unending stream of histories, biographies, diaries, collections of letters, novels, and pictorial presentations has left us with what might be termed an embarrassment of riches—particularly regarding the great battles and leaders of the war.

And yet, there are some aspects of the great struggle about which little has been written. Southern California during the Civil War is a case in point. Although several creditable studies of California's part in the conflict have appeared in recent years, most of these concentrate on the northern half of the state, San Francisco in particular. We are left with a sentence or paragraph here and there to remind us that Confederate sentiment was strong in the southern half of the state, that the California Column marched through the region, that the Dan Showalter party was captured trying to escape to the Confederacy; and with such misinformation as the story that the Confederate flag flew over Los Angeles and that Catalina was seized to forestall a rebel plot.

The purpose of this monograph is to sketch life in Los Angeles and southern California during the years 1860 into 1865, covering the approach of conflict and the conflict itself.

The narrative form is utilized, with digressions on social, economic, political, and military matters that need more attention and background than pure narrative can give. The author has relied heavily on contemporary newspapers—the *Los Angeles Star* and the *Southern News*—and other eyewitness accounts to shed light on Los Angeles during the Civil War period. Hopefully, this effort is one small step toward alleviating the observation of the late W. W. Robinson, Los Angeles historian extraordinary, that no adequate adult history of Los Angeles has yet appeared.[1] Before such a history can be written, many more detailed studies of episodes in the city's pageant need to be undertaken.

One of the pronounced shortcomings of local history is that it too often suffers from provincialism, or myopic vision on the part of the local historian. It is all too easy for the city or county historian, deeply immersed in the past events of his community or region, to fail to integrate the local story with the larger drama of state and nation. Fortunately, this writer faced no such handicap in uncovering the story of Los Angeles in Civil War days. Most of the issues and many of the problems of the city during the years 1860–1865 related closely to state and national happenings.

The author expresses the deepest gratitude to the men and women of the Henry E. Huntington Library, the Los Angeles Public Library, and the U.C.L.A. Library, where most of the research was undertaken. Special thanks are extended to Dr. Edwin H. Carpenter of the Huntington Library for reading the manuscript and offering constructive criticism.

J. W. R.

Costa Mesa, California
April 21, 1976

[1] W. W. Robinson, *Los Angeles: A Profile* (Norman: University of Oklahoma Press, 1968), p. 125.

CONTENTS

ILLUSTRATIONS

Figures

Maps

[11]

LOS ANGELES IN CIVIL WAR DAYS

ABBREVIATIONS
used in the footnotes and bibliography

C.H.S.—California Historical Society
H.S.S.C.—Historical Society of Southern California
P.H.R—Pacific Historical Review
O.R.—The War of the Rebellion: A Compilation
of the Official Records of the Union and
Confederate Armies

LOS ANGELES IN 1860

Viewed from the perspective of today's sprawling metropolis, it is difficult to visualize Los Angeles as it appeared more than a century ago. But let us try.[1] As a start, we must clear away all but an insignificant dozen or so of the present structures, all the paved highways, and most of the vegetation, and place in their stead a few rows of low adobes and several two-story brick buildings, facing an irregular pattern of dusty streets. The heart of the town is the Plaza, a small rectangular clearing dating from Spanish days. Around the Plaza cluster the Catholic church and several adobe structures. Southward, along Main and Los Angeles streets, the town's major thoroughfares, is the business district. Here, a score of newly-constructed brick buildings loom conspicuously above the flat-roofed adobe skyline. Northwest from the Plaza is "Sonora-town," the main residential section. A short block southeast is the infamous Calle de los Negros—"Nigger Alley"—a real-life den of iniquity made up of cheap saloons, gambling dens and bawdy houses. The town's adobe "sub-

[1] The description of Los Angeles in 1860 is largely derived from the following sources: Lynn Bowman, *Los Angeles: Epic of A City* (Berkeley: Howell-North Books, 1974); J. Gregg Layne, *Annals of Los Angeles* (San Francisco: California Historical Society, 1935); Harris Newmark, *Sixty Years in Southern California*, 4th edition, ed. by W. W. Robinson (Los Angeles: Zeitlin & Ver Brugge, 1970); Charles Dwight Willard, *The Herald's History of Los Angeles* (Los Angeles: Kingsley, Barnes & Neuner Co., 1901); and various issues of the *Los Angeles Star*, 1860.

urbs" extend southward to the vicinity of Sixth Street. All of this occupies but a few square miles, wedged tightly between Elysian Hill and the low bluffs above the Los Angeles riverbed.

East of town, on both sides of the river, are a number of small vineyards bordered by willow thickets. William Wolfskill's orange orchard, on the southeast edge of the community, is an island of green amid drab surroundings. Westward, extending all the way to Ballona Creek and the Pacific, and south to New San Pedro, are "The Plains," a monotony of flat grassland broken here and there with low hills. Looming starkly on the northern horizon are the olive-green San Gabriel Mountains.

The people of Los Angeles—4,399 of them according to the 1860 census—are predominantly Spanish speaking. A few belong to the land-rich, cultured California families, but most of the Spanish language element are ex-miners, laborers, ranch hands or drifters, low on the socio-economic scale.

A good part of the town's social practices reflect the Spanish and Mexican background. Christmas and Easter celebrations feature music, dancing, drama, and processions. Weddings are festive occasions.

In the tradition associated with its Hispanic heritage, life, in many respects, is casual in Los Angeles. The afternoon siesta is still popular. The post office consists of a soap box, subdivided like a pigeon house, from which citizens help themselves to their own mail. Buildings and houses are unnumbered, designated simply as "across from the Bella Union," or "near the Express Office." There are no banks; financial transactions are usually simple and personal.

Although the Spanish-speaking culture is still numerically dominant, it is fast retreating before the onslaught of Anglo-American industry and aggressiveness. "Gringos" newly arrived from Texas and states east of the Mississippi, or down from the gold fields of the Mother Lode, along with a handful of Americans of longer residence, are the culture-bearers of the new civilization. They bring with them new social practices, new laws, a new basis for land ownership, and business acumen.

Already, brick is replacing adobe as the standard building material. On city streets, the spike-wheeled wagon is now more often seen than the ox-drawn, cumbersome *carreta*. Perhaps most indicative of all, the year 1860 witnesses the last bull fight in Los Angeles. The sport is outlawed after a child is trampled in the ring. Almost simultaneously, the town's first baseball team is organized.

Foreigners make up a small but significant part of the population. Largest is the French community numbering more than 400, many engaged in wine-making. There is a small but active German element, and a handful of Chinese.

At rock bottom of the social and economic scale are the Indians, more than a thousand of them groveling for a miserable living in and around Los Angeles. They work in the vineyards and on the nearby ranchos during the week. Saturday afternoon, having secured pay, many of them drift to Calle de los Negros to indulge in drink and carouse. Afterwards, the drunken Indians are arrested, put on chain gangs, auctioned off to the highest bidder, and forced to work off their sentence on various projects about town. In 1860 their numbers are greatly decreased from ten years previous—victims of debauchery, the slave-labor market, the white man's diseases, and the destruction of their native culture. In another decade they will be almost totally liquidated as a people.[2]

Although the extreme lawlessness of the mid-1850s has somewhat receded, Los Angeles in 1860 is still burdened with a high rate of crime and violence. Drunken brawls, robberies,

[2] This Indian slave labor policy is generally believed to have passed from the scene in the late 1850s, but Newmark (p. 286) witnessed it going strong in 1860. For a vivid and shocking account of the demise of the Los Angeles Indians, see W. W. Robinson's *The Indians of Los Angeles: Story of the Liquidation of a People* (Los Angeles: Glen Dawson, 1952).

and murders are so commonplace that, unless the victim is someone of importance, the crimes receive only fleeting mention in the press. Justice is often administered in the form of a necktie party, hosted by self-styled vigilantes.[3]

The building boom of the late 1850s has tapered off, but construction goes on. Los Angeles is well underway at losing her cow-town image with such commercial centers as Abel Stearns' Arcadia Block, on the southwest corner of Los Angeles and Arcadia streets; John Temple's Temple Block, in the wedge between Main and Spring streets; and Mellus Row, on Los Angeles Street between Aliso and First. The largest building in town is the new Court House, surmounted by a unique—some say grotesque—clock tower, just south of Temple Block.

The city boasts three hotels, all on Main Street. First and foremost is Dr. James B. Winston's Bella Union, recently remodeled and now two stories high. The Bella Union's dining room is advertised as "one of the finest in all California." Dinnertime is signaled by the blowing of a shrill steam whistle on the hotel roof, at which time prospective diners scurry from all over town to occupy tables. Across the street is the Lafayette Hotel, and a block south the United States Hotel, both of them two stories.

Angelenos seeking entertainment, good food and spirits—assuming they do not wish to stoop to the debauchery of Nigger Alley—can choose between several elegant establishments. Already mentioned is the Bella Union's dining room. The Mongomery Saloon, a block north on Main Street, offers fine liquors (25 cents a drink) and a billiard parlor, where matches are often arranged for a stake of several hundred dollars. Charles Kaiser's Tivoli Garden on Wolfskill Road,

---

[3] City historian Charles Dwight Willard claims that 35 lynchings occurred in Los Angeles between 1850 and 1870, more than four times the number credited to the San Francisco Vigilance Committees. See Willard, p. 280. A more recent and scholarly study of Los Angeles vigilantism is Robert W. Blew's "Vigilantism in Los Angeles, 1835-1874," *Southern California Quarterly*, Spring 1972.

one of the most popular pleasure resorts, provides German beer, music, and dancing on Sunday afternoons. Ramon Alexander, a former French seaman, hosts the Round House at Third and Main, a high-class saloon with a garden in the rear. Emile Bordenave offers excellent French dinners at his Louisiana Coffee Saloon. Roast duck and oysters are the house specialties, the charge fifty cents a meal. Bordenave also serves a "one bit plate" (twelve and one-half cents). Victor Beaudry and Damien Marchessault run the only ice cream saloon in town, offering "iced wine, cobblers and ice cream to your full satisfaction." The ice is packed down from the mountains on muleback, then shipped by wagon to Los Angeles.

1860 sees the birth of the theater in Los Angeles. John Temple presents "The Great Star Company of Stark and Ryer," a visiting troupe of actors, in his large hall over the City Market.

The cattle industry, although past its Golden Age in southern California and beset with a number of problems, is still the premier economic enterprise in Los Angeles. An 1860 census reveals 78,000 head of cattle in the county, distributed on a number of large ranchos in the Los Angeles Basin and San Gabriel Valley. The leading ranchero and richest man in Los Angeles is Abel Stearns, a long-time resident who married into the Bandini family. Stearns, whose Los Angeles home is known as *El Palacio*, owns several important tracts in town as well as vast holdings to the southeast, made up primarily of Ranchos Los Alamitos, Las Bolsas, and Los Coyotes. Second in land holdings to Stearns is "Juan Largo" Temple, proprietor of Rancho Los Cerritos and other tracts. Benjamin Wilson and Dr. John S. Griffin of Rancho San Pasqual, William Workman of Rancho La Puente, Francis Temple of Rancho de Merced, and the Lugo family (Antonio Maria Lugo died in early 1860) of Rancho San Antonio are other major land owners. But the era of the "Cattle on a

Thousand Hills" is fast drawing to a close. The industry is already feeling the pinch of declining cattle prices, questionable land titles, ruinous interest rates, and drought.

Next to cattle, the production of grapes and wine is the most lucrative industry in Los Angeles. There are some 2,000 acres of vineyards in the county. 66,000 cases of wine are shipped out of Los Angeles to San Francisco and the eastern market in 1860.[4] Frenchmen dominate the local viticulture industry: Jean Louis Vignes, Jean-Louis and Pierre Sainsevain, and Emile and Theophile Vache are the leading wine producers.

Oranges are another profitable industry. Out of an estimated 2,500 orange trees in California in 1860, three-fourths of them are in Los Angeles County,[5] and most of these are tended by William Wolfskill.

Industrial development in Los Angeles is in its infancy. All of the town's industrial establishments are minor enterprises employing at most a dozen men. John Goller, here since 1849, is Los Angeles' leading blacksmith and wagon maker. He charges $16 to shoe a horse. His trim wagons, manufactured in his large shop on Los Angeles Street, sell throughout the state. Los Angeles also boasts the Eagle Flour Mill, a furniture and cabinet shop, a tannery, and even a brewery to compete with the French wines.

Water is a major concern. The *zanjas* (irrigation ditches), relics of Spanish days, still criss-cross town, but they are insufficient for the growing city's needs and pose a sanitation problem. Presently, the water comes from the Los Angeles River and springs north of town. A large water wheel hoists the water into a master *zanja*, which carries it to a brick reservoir in the Plaza. From here, iron pipes recently installed take the water down Main and Los Angeles streets into the business district. The system, built by William

[4] Willard, p. 294.
[5] *Ibid.*

Dryden, is an improvement over the old method but remains inadequate.

The town is governed by an elected mayor and common council. Henry Mellus, a transplanted New Englander who came to California with Richard Henry Dana on the brig *Pilgrim*, is mayor most of the year—until his untimely death the day after Christmas. Chairman of the County Board of Supervisors is Abel Stearns. Maryland-born Benjamin Hayes is Judge of the Southern District of California, which encompasses Los Angeles and San Diego counties. Judge Hayes, a highly respected figure about town, spends much of his time traveling his judicial circuit.

Two newspapers serve the community. Henry Hamilton pilots the highly partisan *Los Angeles Star*, published weekly since 1851. C. R. Conway and Alonzo Waite publish the new *Semi-Weekly Southern News*. Readers are treated to several columns of national and world news (usually a week or two late), goings on about town, advertisements of local and San Francisco business enterprises, occasional lines of poetry, and—in the *Star*—outspoken and frequently vitriolic political opinions.

Communication with the outside world, even with other southern California communities, is difficult and painfully slow. Abominable dirt roads, becoming impassable quagmires after rain, connect Los Angeles with El Monte and San Bernardino to the east, the German colony of Anaheim to the southeast, and Phineas Banning's New San Pedro to the south. The leading stage and freight man is Banning, patriarch of the southern county, whose cumbersome wagons carry everything from passengers to lumber over most of southern California.

Wells, Fargo & Company maintains an express office in town, frequently the gathering place of those seeking the latest news from the outside world. The company hauls freight, mail, and gold from the nearby San Gabriel Canyon

Mission Church and Plaza, with Sonoratown in background, before 1869

Lafayette Hotel Stage in Nigger Alley, Los Angeles, about 1861

mines to San Francisco. Los Angeles is a stage stop on the Butterfield Overland Stage Line's St. Louis-to-San Francisco route. A passenger St. Louis-bound can get there in twenty bone-jarring days of bumpy riding; San Francisco takes three days. Butterfield's old "mud wagons" have recently been replaced with brightly-painted, better-upholstered Concord coaches. The steamer *Senator* and several smaller schooners ply the waters between San Francisco and New San Pedro, carrying passengers, freight, and mail.

Via the overland stage, the steamer and, toward the end of the year, the telegraph, Los Angeles learns of the momentous events going on in the East. Although the town is not directly involved in the great national crisis of 1860–1861, her citizens show vital interest and express deep concern.

POLITICAL TURMOIL

STREET RALLIES, torchlight parades, band music, cannon salutes, picnics, barbecues, and long-winded oratory—this was
politics, Los Angeles style, 1860. Partisanship ran at a fever
pitch. The oratory was usually enlivened by violent diatribes
against candidates of the rival party. The more unrestrained
and vitriolic the language, the greater was the popularity of
the speaker. The height of local political invective was
reached during a Democratic mass meeting in 1859 when
Colonel Edward J. C. Kewen verbally assaulted J. J. Warner
with the following diatribe, in part: "This trifling fellow,
Warner, is so notoriously corrupt and villainous, as to wholly
exclude him from any consideration except that which
prompts a man to kick a snarling cur that intercepts his path.
The reptile's teeth have been extracted, there is now no ven-
nom in his bite."[1] Warner, of course, answered the attack in
like manner: "A slanderer [Kewen] should be met by the
lash at every street corner and chased into the wilderness to
live among the howling wolves."[2] The verbal battle lasted
two months, with such epithets tossed back and forth as
"truckling slave," "sordid Hessian," "dirty scribbler," and
"skulking traitor."[3]

[1] *Los Angeles Star*, August 3, 1859.
[2] *Southern Vineyard*, August 12, 1859.
[3] See *Star* and *Southern Vineyard*, various issues, July and August 1859.

Los Angeles, looking south from the Court House, about 1867

LOS ANGELES, CAL., THURSDAY, MAY 13, 1869.

Los Angeles County Court House, looking east, 1869

One might reason that a small frontier town, far from the national population centers, both in distance and in notoriously slow communication, would neglect the game of politics. But such was far from the truth. Political interest in state and national issues was acute, as evidenced by the space given these matters in the Los Angeles press. As the sectional controversy developed in the East and the Gwin-Broderick rivalry grew in California, Los Angeles became more and more involved in national and state issues. Many a long-standing friendship was strained and even ruptured over political differences.

Los Angeles was an overwhelmingly Democratic town in the years preceding the Civil War. Until the great Democratic schism of 1860, the party was a runaway winner in every local contest with Whigs, Know-Nothings, and later Republicans. The break in Democratic ranks that developed in the mid-1850s saw the majority of Los Angeles Democrats side with the "Chivalry," as the Southern element in the state called itself. The drift of the Southern states toward secession was greeted with sympathy and understanding by a large part of the local citizenry.

These positive feelings toward the South were only natural. In the 1850s, emigrants from Texas and border slave states poured into southern California, settling in San Diego, San Bernardino, El Monte, as well as Los Angeles. Many leading Los Angeles citizens were natives of slave states: Benjamin Wilson, William Wolfskill, Benjamin Hayes, Dr. John S. Griffin, Colonel Edward J. C. Kewen, Dr. James B. Winston, and J. Lancaster Brent, to name the most influential. Southern California was linked directly with the South by Lieutenant Edward F. Beale's military wagon road, completed in 1858, and the Butterfield Overland Stage Line, opened the same year. Of no little importance in southern California's ties with the South was the Federal patronage: a succession of Democratic presidents had filled all Federal appointive positions with political partisans, usually chosen by the "Chivalry" wing of the party.[4]

Of no small importance in perpetuating the Southern Democratic persuasion of Los Angeles in the years before the Civil War was Henry Hamilton, outspoken editor of the _Los Angeles Star_. The _Star_, Los Angeles' first newspaper, was founded in 1851 and run by a succession of mediocre editors until Hamilton took over the paper in January, 1856. In the ensuing two or three years, Henry Hamilton transformed the _Star_ into a sound and thriving journal with an unusually high degree of literary acumen for a small town frontier newspaper.

Henry Hamilton was a native of Londonderry, Ireland who emigrated to the United States in 1848, trained as a printers' apprentice. He journeyed to California the following year and tried his hand in gold mining. In this endeavor he was less than successful. In 1851 he drifted into San Francisco and became a reporter and writer for the _Public Balance_, one of the small, short-lived gold rush journals of the Bay city. Following the _Public Balance's_ demise later in 1851, Hamilton and two associates returned to the Mother Lode country and founded the _Calaveras Journal_ at Mokelumne Hill. Five years later he sold his interest in the _Journal_ and moved to Los Angeles, where he commenced his editorship of the _Star_.

Henry Hamilton had more than a mere journalistic attitude toward the newspapers he published. He possessed a cosmopolitan interest in things literary: printing essays, stories, and poetry as well as news reports. His most valued contributor in the early days of the _Star_ was "Ina," who later as Ina Donna Coolbrith, became the poet laureate of Cali-

[4] For a discussion of southern California's pre-Civil War ties with the South, see Helen B. Walters, "Confederates in Southern California," _H.S.S.C. Quarterly_, March 1953; Percival J. Cooney, "Southern California in Civil War Days," _Annual Publication of the H.S.S.C._, 1924; and George William Beattie, _Heritage of the Valley: San Bernardino's First Century_ (Oakland: Biobooks, 1951), pp. 350–351.

fornia. The *Star* contained advertisements for learned Eastern journals such as the *Atlantic Monthly*, and often reprinted articles from these journals. Hamilton's interest was world-wide, as he often editorialized on affairs and conditions in England, France, Naples, and even China and Japan. There was little of importance in the cultural or scientific world that escaped his scrutiny.

But the passion foremost in the mind of Henry Hamilton was reserved for things political. And in politics, he was a rabid Democrat with pronounced Southern sympathies. Seldom has the Democratic party enjoyed the support of so strenuous an advocate. William B. Rice, in his history of the *Star*, writes of Hamilton: "His talents in the use of invective he devoted to the Democratic cause. He was a far western outpost of that party's organization; he and others like him made California into a Democratic pocket borough. Hamilton paid little attention to local events; his eye was on the horizon, and he stood Jovelike—according to a borrowed metaphor—hurling his bolts at apostate Democrats and Black Republicans. He made each issue of the *Star* a tract, each editorial a party argument."[5]

There is nothing in Hamilton's background to indicate why he became such a strong supporter of the South and a negrophobe. As far as is known, he never visited the South nor witnessed slavery in action, yet historians of the pre-Civil War period would be hard-put to find a stronger advo- of the "peculiar institution" anywhere. Hamilton had been at the helm of the *Star* for only a few months when his negro-phobia became evident to his readers. Upon discovering that some members of the Los Angeles common council were Republican sympathizers, he promptly labeled the council "nigger-worshippers" who had unfurled "the abolition flag." The new Republican Party, with its alleged abolitionist be-

[5] William B. Rice, *The Los Angeles Star, 1851–1864: The Beginnings of Journalism in Southern California* (Berkeley: University of California Press, 1947), p. 121.

liefs, was an anathema to Hamilton. The *Star's* editor labeled the Republicans "the most dangerous threat to American institutions since George III."[6]

Hamilton's political enthusiasm was put to a severe test by the growing split in the Democratic Party. The national schism over the slavery issue was a cloud fast rising on the horizon, and it manifested itself in 1859 in the big fight over the admission of Kansas as a slave or free state. The Buchanan administration favored admitting the strife-torn territory under the so-called Lecompton Constitution, drafted by proslavery advocates. Democrats who opposed the extension of slavery rallied behind Senator Stephen A. Douglas in opposing Kansas' entry under this constitution. In California, this Kansas debate was echoed in the intense rivalry between the state's two senators, William M. Gwin and David C. Broderick. Gwin and his "Chivalry" followers supported the Buchanan administration, while Broderick stubbornly fought the president. The dispute was heightened by the extremely bitter personal rivalry between the two men, and the resulting political feud divided California Democrats into two angry and vociferous camps.

In Los Angeles, the *Star* strongly backed the "regular" Democrats against the Broderick faction. The local party was badly split from 1857 on, with increasing vehemence every year. Los Angeles had its own Gwin-Broderick clash in the form of an intense feud, mentioned earlier, between Colonel Edward J. C. Kewen of the Chivalry faction and J. J. Warner of the Broderick wing. The Chivalry won the 1859 election and Hamilton was overjoyed, saying the results would "gladden the patriotic heart of James Buchanan."[7]

A week later the news reached Los Angeles that Broderick had been killed in a duel with Judge David S. Terry. The town was stunned, and some citizens wept in the streets.

---

[6] Los Angeles *Star*, August 16 and 30, November 1, 1856.
[7] *Ibid.*, September 17, 1859.

Hamilton, who during the campaign had villified Broderick, expressed sorrow in "the untimely death of this distinguished and estimable gentleman."[8] Broderick now became a martyr to the anti-slavery Democrats of the state.

Another issue that deeply concerned Los Angeles was the proposal, first voiced in 1850, to divide the state. The idea of splitting California was popular in the southern counties, where a feeling was strong that San Francisco unfairly dominated the state government. In February 1859, Los Angeles County Assemblyman Andrés Pico introduced a resolution to create the "Territory of Colorado" out of the five southern counties of San Luis Obispo, Santa Barbara, Los Angeles, San Diego, and San Bernardino.[9] The Legislature approved the bill in April and called for a vote on the proposal by the southern counties in the next general election. The measure passed with an overwhelming margin in the September vote; in Los Angeles County alone the count was 1,467 in favor of state division and 441 opposed.[10] But because of the growing national crisis and the Civil War, the plan was killed in Congress. Were it not for the Civil War, California would very likely be in two parts today.[11]

The year 1860 opened with an ominous lull in Los Angeles. Citizens were concerned with the recent floods that had damaged the Plaza church and other buildings and streets.

Los Angeles had a new newspaper to replace the *Southern Vineyard*, which folded when J. J. Warner went off to the state assembly. C. R. Conway and Alonzo Waite's *Semi-Weekly Southern News* made its appearance on January 18th and announced that it would be a politically independent

[8] *Ibid.*, September 24, 1859.

[9] Orange, Riverside, and Imperial counties did not exist in 1859.

[10]*Star*, September 17, 1859. For a discussion of the state division issue as it affected Los Angeles, see Rice, pp. 175–176.

[11] Robert Glass Cleland, *From Wilderness to Empire* (New York: Alfred A. Knopf, 1944), pp. 300–301.

sheet and report the news as it saw fit.[12] The *Star* greeted its new competitor with silence.

The town abruptly rejoiced in the streets when it heard the news that John G. Downey, one of its own, had replaced Milton S. Latham as governor of California when the latter resigned to accept a Senate seat. Downey, a native of Ireland, had come to California in 1849 with $10 in his pocket. He opened a drug store in Los Angeles the following year, the only establishment of its kind between San Francisco and San Diego, and accumulated $10,000 in three years. He also delved into cattle raising and real estate, gathering a handsome fortune by 1859. He owned about 75,000 acres near the present site of Downey.[13] In politics he was a fence-straddling Democrat, more closely allied with the Chivalry than the Broderick wing, but not enough so to suit the *Star*. Nevertheless, the *Star* shared the town's happiness: "A salute of one hundred guns was fired from the Plaza, in honor of the new governor, and in the evening a torch light procession paraded the town, headed by a band of music, carrying transparencies inscribed 'Senator Latham,' 'Governor Downey,' and 'Our Union.' "[14]

Local politics took the spotlight in May when Henry Mellus was elected Mayor. "Next day, he and the other City officers paraded our streets in a four-horse stagecoach with a brass band. The Mayor-elect and his *confreres* were stuffed inside the hot, decorated vehicle, while the puffing musicians bounced up and down on the swaying top outside, like popcorn in a frying pan."[15]

But deep in many minds was the foreboding news from the East. The *Star* expressed outrage over John Brown's raid on Harper's Ferry, worried over the threat of disunion, and ridi-

[12] Rice, pp. 140–141.
[13] Hubert Howe Bancroft, *History of California*, Vol. VII (San Francisco: The History Co., 1890), p. 279, footnote.
[14] *Star*, January 21, 1860.
[15] Newmark, p. 268.

culed Kentucky Senator Crittenden's plan for a Great National Union Party.[16] Week after week, the front pages of the two Los Angeles newspapers were filled with stories of the national crisis.

The *Star* quoted and approved ex-Governor Weller's suggestion that California, in the event of disunion, "not go with the South or the North, but here upon the shores of the Pacific found a mighty republic, which may in the end be the greatest of all."[17] The Pacific Republic plan would soon become a favorite topic of Henry Hamilton.

Myron Norton, Chivalry Democrat, represented Los Angeles County at the Democratic State Convention in Sacramento in March. The convention chose California delegates to the National Convention, to be held in Charleston, South Carolina, and passed resolutions upholding the Buchanan policies, opposing Stephen Douglas, and supporting Daniel S. Dickinson as the choice of California Democracy for president.[18] The Chivalry was in command—for the last time.

The *Star* held great hopes for the success of the Charleston convention. "At no former period have we observed so great a unanimity among the people, to accept the nominee of a National Convention as the exponent of the will of the people, as on the present occasion. The issue is the fate of the Union."[19]

The news of the disruption of the Charleston convention came as a great shock to Los Angeles Democrats. The *Star* heard the news with surprise and dismay and urged reconciliation of the opposing factions when the Democrats tried again in Baltimore: "If a reconciliation be not consummated, and all do not work harmoniously together, the destinies of our country will be committed, for the next four years, to the Black Republican Party."[20]

[16] *Star*, February 25, 1860.
[17] *Ibid.*
[18] *Ibid.*, March 10, 1860.
[19] *Ibid.*, April 7, 1860.
[20] *Ibid.*, May 19, 1860.

Los Angeles' small but dedicated group of Republicans were heartened by the Democratic break-up. The "corporal's guard among us"—what the *Star* called the local Republicans—began to drum up recruits, chiefly among disenchanted Democrats.[21]

The Democrats met once more in Baltimore, but were no closer to settling their differences than before. In June the deeply divided party made Stephen Douglas its presidential nominee, whereupon the Southern delegates walked out and, in a rival convention, selected Vice President John Breckenridge of Kentucky as their presidential nominee. The Democratic schism was complete.

William Seward of New York was the pre-convention favorite to win the Republican nomination, but the Republicans, meeting in Chicago in May, surprised almost everyone by choosing Abraham Lincoln of Illinois and Hannibal Hamlin of Maine as their standard-bearers. Few in Los Angeles knew much about Lincoln. The *Star* called the Republicans "crazy as March hares" and predicted that "The Democracy will be almost without an opponent in November."[22]

In June the Los Angeles Republicans, their numbers still small but growing since the Democratic dissension, organized a club and rented a hall in Temple Block as their headquarters.[23] Among the leading Lincoln supporters in town were Isaac Hartman, Juan Sepúlveda, Manuel Requena, Felipe Lugo, and O. W. Childs.

The local Republicans received a boost when John C. Fremont visited Los Angeles on July 31st. He was given a 21-gun salute in the Plaza, then feted that evening at the Bella Union. Republicans for miles around, including the staunch Unionist Phineas Banning of New San Pedro, journeyed in to greet the famed but slightly tarnished pathfinder.[24]

21 *Ibid.*, May 26, 1860.
22 *Ibid.*, June 9, 1860.
23 *Ibid.*, June 30, 1860.
24 *Ibid.*, August 4, 1860, and Newmark, p. 272.

The local Democrats, like their state and national brethren, were badly split. The *Star* came out strong for Breckenridge and blamed Douglas for the party schism,[25] but many Democrats failed to follow suit. Governor Downey disappointed many of his Los Angeles friends by coming out for Douglas.[26]

The Los Angeles County Democratic Central Committee met at the Court House early in August amid rumors of dissension. Two resolutions were offered: one by General Ezra Drown to support Douglas, the other by Benjamin Wilson to back Breckenridge. The motion to support Breckenridge was carried by a vote of nine to one, whereupon General Drown rose from his seat, announced that he would have nothing to do further with the committee and walked out.[27]

The Douglas supporters called their own meeting a few days later. Among those present and espousing the cause of the "Little Giant" and Northern Democracy were Assemblyman J. J. Warner, Mayor Henry Mellus, and ex-Committeeman Ezra Drown.[28]

A four-ring political circus was complete with the formation in Los Angeles of the Bell and Everett Club to back the candidates of the compromise National Union Party. Dr. Thomas Foster was elected chairman of the rump group.[29]

Political hoop-la now embraced Los Angeles almost every night, with bombastic oratory, tar-barrel burning, torchlight parades, loud music, and cannon salutes frequently breaking the stillness of the night air. One unfamiliar with the ongoing campaign might have believed the town at war: the Republican 21-gun salute for Fremont was dwarfed by the booming of 100 guns in honor of Breckenridge. The Breckenridge Club held mass rallies in front of the Montgomery Saloon every Tuesday evening, followed by noisy torchlight

[25] *Star*, July 21, 1860.
[26] *Ibid.*, August 11, 1860.
[27] *Ibid.*, August 11, 1860.
[28] *Ibid.*, August 18, 1860.
[29] *Ibid.*, August 25, 1860.

Bella Union Hotel, Los Angeles, 1865
(East side of Main Street
between Commercial and Arcadia Streets)

processions up Main Street to the Plaza. Colonel Kewen was often called upon to deliver one of his patented harangues. Senator Latham stopped off in town enroute to Washington and spoke for two hours to the Breckenridgites before the Montgomery Saloon; the *Star* called his address "forceful and eloquent"—which meant that Hamilton agreed with it—given to an assemblage "by far the greatest of any which has taken place during the campaign."[30] Douglas supporters congregated weekly in front of the Lafayette Hotel for an evening's entertainment of partisan oratory and martial music. The Republicans, outnumbered but determined not to be outstaged, marched around Temple Block before listening to Isaac Hartman expound on the virtues of Lincoln and Hamlin.[31]

A month before election day, the *Star* informed its readers that "politics are now the chief topic of conversation, and the discussions sometimes become decidedly animated, if not heated. Bets are frequently offered and taken on the general result of the election.[32] One anonymous Breckenridge Democrat placed the following ad in the *Star*:

> $1000 TO WIN OR LOSE!
> I will bet one thousand dollars, $500 that George W. Gift is elected Assemblyman and $500 that A. J. King is elected Assemblyman, both bets taken together. For particulars apply at this office.
>
> A DEMOCRAT [33]

In the midst of the campaign, the telegraph line between San Francisco and Los Angeles was completed. On October 8th, the first messages were flashed back and forth between the two cities. That night there was a gala celebration at the

[30] *Ibid.*, October 13, 1860.
[31] *Ibid.*, September 8, 1860.
[32] *Ibid.*, October 27, 1860.
[33] *Ibid.*, November 3, 1860.

Bella Union to celebrate the historic hook-up. No longer was Los Angeles quite so isolated. News from the East that formerly took ten to twelve days to reach town now galloped across the country via Pony Express, then was wired south, usually in about six days but sometimes longer. The fee for receiving news via telegraph was $100 per month; neither the *Star* nor the *Southern News* felt it could afford this. The problem was solved when Phineas Banning, the Newmarks, and several other local businessmen subscribed the $100 a month so that dispatches would reach Los Angeles quickly.[34] The telegraph line suffered frequent breakdowns, particularly during the crucial early months of 1861, but on the whole Los Angeles benefitted from the new mode of communication.

As election day neared, the *Star* saw ominous forebodings in events back East. Ohio and Pennsylvania went Republican in October elections, prompting Hamilton to plead, "Now when the black waters of Republicanism are surging over the land, threatening to engulf the sacred ark of our rights and liberty, let the Democracy stand forward and present a solid barrier to its further progress."[35]

In the final issue before election day, Hamilton once more begged Democrats to stop the "Black Republican" tide: "A crisis, a momentous crisis is at hand. Clouds lower on the horizon, such as never before darkened the career of the country. A faction whose tenets lead to the subversion and overthrow of the Constitution, vaunt that they will carry out their principles to the bitter end, and that, we all know, is the disruption of this glorious Confederacy. Democrats, will you permit the success of that party? On you rests the defense of the Constitution—the perpetuity of the Union."[36]

The *Southern News*, on the other hand, maintained neutrality. The paper called the election "the greatest struggle

[34] *Ibid.*, October 13, 1860; and Newmark, p. 284.
[35] *Star*, October 27, 1860.
[36] *Ibid.*, November 3, 1860.

Abel Stearns

Joseph Lancaster Brent

John S. Griffin, M.D.

B. D. Wilson

J. J. Warner

Edward J. C. Kewen

William McKee

Henry Hamilton

since 1840," but considered all the national candidates able men and failed to see any immediate danger to the Union,[37] a strange complacency in the midst of storm!

Election day passed rather quietly in Los Angeles. Both of the Democratic parties scurried around to rouse their respective supporters. The *Southern News* reported carriages flying about town, bringing tardy voters to the polls at the Montgomery Saloon.[38]

Next day the ballots were counted. Los Angeles was safe for Breckenridge, despite the Lincoln victory and Democratic disaster that appeared to be taking hold elsewhere. The big surprise locally was that the Douglas candidates for state assembly, Abel Stearns and Murray Morrison, defeated the Breckenridge slate.

Before the final national returns were known, the *Star* ran a rather optimistic and myopic editorial concerning the local vote: "Upon the great national issues that divide the Union, we have met the enemy, and in this county, conquered them. Whatever disaster may have occured elsewhere, here our glorious banner flutters in victory."[39] Then, in a bit of twisted logic, Hamilton claimed that the Breckenridge candidates for assembly "suffered a defeat more glorious than a victory."[40]

The Republicans, although not winning a single local contest, were ecstatic. They gathered in Temple Block and wandered up to the Plaza, singing the praises of Abe Lincoln.[41]

The final election tally for the Los Angeles precinct showed the following presidential vote:[42]

> Breckenridge 686
> Douglas 494
> Lincoln 350
> Bell 201

[37] *Southern News*, November 2, 1860.
[38] *Ibid.*, November 9, 1860.
[39] *Star*, November 10, 1860.
[40] *Ibid.*,
[41] *Southern News*, November 9, 1860.
[42] *Star*, November 17, 1860.

The *Star* was strangely silent on political issues for a month. The telegraphic news poured in daily from the East, telling of the national crisis and the South's secession threats. In December, Hamilton expressed dismay and regret at what the South was planning, but argued it was not to blame. For California, he thought the proposed Republic of the Pacific was a strong possibility.[43]

[43] *Ibid.*, December 15, 1860.

THE JUDICIAL ELECTION.

THE 21st OF OCTOBER.

(The District consists of the counties of San Diego, San Bernardino, Los Angeles, Santa Barbara, and San Luis Obispo.)

To the People of the First Judicial District.

I am a candidate for District Judge, holding the same principle I expressed in the years 1852 and 1858, that—"the office of *Judge* should be maintained free forever from any influence of mere party politics;" which was then endorsed by a majority of fourteen hundred votes.

Such is the true spirit of our amended Constitution, in the separation of the Judicial from the General election. And an example, most worthy of admiration and imitation, has been given by the judiciary, Federal and State, throughout the rest of the Union; preserving ever a calm silence, save in the cases duly tried before their Courts, upon "the vexed questions" of the war and particular measures of governmental policy. Thus their INTEGRITY remains untouched, whatever convulsions the hour may threaten. Clamor pushed on by zeal and impatience, no doubt often calls them into the political arena; but, unmoved they keep within their own sphere, and have firmly held their INDEPENDENCE and IMPARTIALITY. Nor do the reflection and reason of the country complain of them.

It encourages me now, to observe the same wise and just moderation ruling public sentiment in this District, as always heretofore.

For myself, I cheerfully leave my official acts to the kind consideration of *the mass of the people.* For your confidence I have had so long, I feel deeply grateful; your renewal of it, at a critical period, would be a very high honor conferred upon me. In return, if my past life of nearly fourteen years among you prove anything, I can safely promise—FIDELITY TO THE CONSTITUTION AND THE LAWS.

Respectfully,

BENJAMIN HAYES.

Los Angeles, 1863.

John G. Downey

RUMBLINGS OF WAR

THE YEAR 1861 dawned dark and foreboding. South Carolina's secession, followed by the defection of other states in the deep South, filled the pages of the *Star* and *Southern News*. The Union appeared to be dissolving with a rapidity no one expected, and local citizens were in a disturbed state of mind.[1]

Judge Benjamin Hayes expressed the uneasy feelings of many. Hayes had long been a Chivalry Democrat; yet, with troubled mind, he had voted for Douglas in the late election. He wrote to a friend in January, "The North I consider to be wrong on the vital issue, and the South right, I think. And still, like yourself, I am for the Union." He was deeply disturbed over the danger facing the nation: "I can with difficulty drive from my mind the thought that in a few days more, we shall be plunged into the horrors of a fratricidal war." He spoke of the calm local reaction to the crisis: "In this vicinity the impending danger is spoken of by everybody, without warm discussion; in fact, as if by general understanding, irritating points of controversy are avoided. . . . We go about our business, manifesting not the slightest apprehension for ourselves. Yet we look every moment for the commencement of hostilities. None, I suppose, would be surprised to learn tomorrow or the next day that Fort Sumter

[1] Newmark, p. 289.

had been stormed—or that the Capital had been taken." The Judge closed his letter with an expression of love for the Union: "How I wish I could hear a full band strike up the Star-Spangled Banner! My own state [Maryland] gave it to the nation."[2]

Although there was widespread regret at the break-up of the Union, many—probably a clear majority—in Los Angeles sympathized with the South's course of action. Writing to his sister in February, Judge Hayes stated that "the tone of the people here is Southern to a greater extent than might be supposed in the present controversy."[3] The *Star* saw the Confederacy as a fixed fact, the separation of the Union as complete, and blamed the fanaticism of the North: "Much as we deplore the disruption of the Union, we cannot but admit that the South, if she could not have her rights in it, is justified in maintaining them out of it." Hamilton saw Lincoln as facing an impossible task: "We will not at all be astonished to see him denounced by his own party before long."[4] The same issue of the paper carried the complete text of Jefferson Davis' inaugural address. The *Southern News*, still not unduly alarmed, believed "the erring states" would be allowed to go in peace and saw little prospect of war.[5]

The *Star* once more advocated that California and the other western states and territories form a Pacific Republic, allied with neither North or South. Neutrality, Hamilton believed, would preserve the state from internal disorder, and, besides, California's interests were not involved in the quarrel. "Peace is unquestionably our policy; if any are indisposed to abide thereby, they had better transport themselves to the scenes of war and blood."[6]

[2] *Pioneer Notes from the Diaries of Judge Benjamin Hayes, 1849–1875* (Los Angeles: privately printed, 1929), pp. 251–255.
[3] *Ibid.*, p. 256.
[4] *Star*, March 16, 1861.
[5] *Southern News*, February 27, 1861.
[6] *Star*, January 5, May 11, 1861.

A number of volunteer military companies were organized in Los Angeles and surrounding areas during February and March, in keeping with Governor Downey's call for 5,000 volunteer militia to preserve the public order. Early in February, the "Los Angeles Greys" were formed at a meeting in the Court House. Immediately the militia unit petitioned the state adjutant general for arms and ammunition. The following month saw the birth of the 80-man "Los Angeles Mounted Rifles," presided over by George W. Gift, assisted by Alonzo Ridley. Both of these gentlemen had strong pro-Southern beliefs; we shall hear more of them later. Out in El Monte, 12 miles east, the "Monte Mounted Rifles" were organized, 70 vigilante-prone "Monte Boys" under the leadership of Frank Green and Andrew King. El Monte, peopled largely by transplanted Texans, was a hotbed of Southern Democracy and a dangerous place for Republicans to venture.[7]

Not all volunteers in these local militia units were Southern sympathizers, but enough were to worry Captain Winfield Scott Hancock, quartermaster of the Army's Southern District of the Department of the Pacific, and the only regular army officer in Los Angeles at the time. Captain Hancock had been stationed in Los Angeles since May 1859. From his office on Main Street near Third, he purchased and distributed food, supplies, and livestock to military posts in southern California and Arizona. Hancock was worried that Southern sympathizers in some of these quasi-military units might attempt to seize his army stores, particularly the guns and ammunition. But for the moment, all he could do was remain vigilant.[8]

[7] *Star*, February 2, March 9, 16, 1861; J. M. Scammell, "Military Units in Southern California," *C.H.S. Quarterly*, September 1950; William F. King, "El Monte, An American Town in Southern California, 1851–1866," *Southern California Quarterly*, December 1971.

[8] Newmark, p. 246–247; Almira Hancock, *Reminiscences of Winfield Scott Hancock by His Wife* (New York: Charles L. Webster & Co., 1887), pp. 59–60.

In late March Lincoln's inaugural address reached Los Angeles. The *Star* thought it contradictory, threatening war and offering peace in the same breath, and called it a failure.[9] The *Southern News*, on the other hand, was finally awakening from its lethargy over the crisis. It liked the speech and believed all Union men would approve it, and predicted Lincoln would do all in his power to conciliate the South without compromising the dignity of his office.[10]

A month after the inauguration, Lincoln's firm hand was felt in southern California, and the *Star* was enraged. The issue was federal patronage. For more than a decade, federal patronage in California had been controlled by Chivalry Democrats working with friendly Democratic administrations in Washington, resulting in a virtual monopoly for Southern-leaning federal office-holders in the state. Now that a Republican administration was in Washington for the first time, California Republican leaders were determined to change this situation. Leland Stanford sailed from San Francisco in January to confer with the president-elect on this matter, and he was joined in the national capital by Edward Baker, late of California but now Republican Senator from Oregon. Together the two met with Lincoln a few days after the inauguration and advised the president on federal appointments in California. The result was that all appointments in the state were filled with men of firm loyalty to the Union.[11]

Local officers appointed by Lincoln were Henry D. Barrows, United States Marshal; K. H. Dimmick, Federal Attorney for the Southern District; Oscar Macy, Customs Collector at San Pedro; and Antonio María Pico, nephew of Pío Pico,

[9] *Star*, March 23, 1861.

[10] *Southern News*, March 27, 1861.

[11] George T. Clark, *Leland Stanford: War Governor of California, Railroad Builder and Founder of Stanford University* (Stanford: Stanford University Press, 1931), pp. 95–99.

Registrar of the Land Office in Los Angeles. Only Dimmick and Barrows were residents of southern California.

The *Star* condemned Lincoln for the appointments, declaring that none of the men were competent, and that Macy and Pico were totally unfamiliar with local problems. Hamilton was particularly incensed that Edward Baker of Oregon had a hand in the selections while California's two senators, both Democrats, were not consulted. "We wonder that Abe . . . didn't expatriate suckers for every office in the State." [12]

The electrifying news of the attack on Fort Sumter required twelve days to reach San Francisco via Pony Express, then was relayed to Los Angeles via telegraph, reaching here on the afternoon of April 24th. The news caused "the most profound sensation," according to the *Star*.[13] The streets of Los Angeles were suddenly filled with excited, milling crowds, expressing mingled feelings of elation and sorrow.[14] Los Angeles threw off its veneer of calm detachment, evident since the beginning of the crisis; the war which almost everyone had talked about but few had really believed would happen was now starkly real, and the effect on emotions was dramatic. Los Angeles, three thousand miles from the seat of conflict, was deeply involved in the martial spirit. And this spirit in the minds and hearts of men surging through the streets was decidedly pro-Southern.

[12] *Star*, April 27, 1861.
[13] *Ibid*
[14] Newmark, p. 294.

HOTBED OF SECESSIONISM

PRESIDENT LINCOLN'S CALL for 75,000 volunteers and a naval blockade to subdue the South unleased a torrent of abuse from the *Star*: "In the clash of arms, the American Constitution has perished. . . . Instead of a Federal Government composed of a Legislative, Judicial and an Executive Department, we find the whole power of government seized by *one man*, and exercised is irresponsibly as by the Czar of Russia."[1]

Secessionists in Los Angeles echoed Hamilton's outrage. The coming of war had unleashed a fury of fundamental emotions. Uncertainty and doubt suddenly vanished in an orgy of popular excitement. Flushed faces, wild eyes, and screaming voices filled the Bella Union and Montgomery Saloon and spilled out into the streets. Angry and excited crowds shouted hurrahs for Jeff Davis and the Confederacy and hurled insults at the Unionists. The Bella Union was the nerve center of secessionist outrage. A few days after the news of Fort Sumter, a huge portrait of General Beauregard was hung in the hotel saloon. Barroom songs, hurriedly composed for the occasion and often sung to the tune of popular ballads, reverberated through the halls and echoed into the streets. Two of the favorite ditties were "We'll Hang Abe Lincoln

[1] *Star*, May 11, 1861.

to a Tree" and "We'll Drive the Bloody Tyrant from Our Dear Native Soil."[2]

The secessionist outburst worried Captain Winfield Scott Hancock, the Army's lone officer in town. After receiving a warning that Southern sympathizers planned to raid his quartermaster stores, Hancock concealed the arms and ammunition under bags of grain and improvised a barricade of wagons and boxes. He assembled a small arsenal of twenty Derringers for his own use, armed his wife, and recruited Union sympathizers to help defend the government property.[3] Amid threatening gestures from secessionists, he was fully prepared to fight it out until help arrived. For a few days—until troops reached Los Angeles from Fort Tejon—it was touch and go. "Probably all that saved the faraway section of southern California for the Union at this critical moment was Hancock's care in seeing that his precious guns, ammunition and supplies were adequately protected," writes Hancock's latest biographer.[4] Although this assessment is almost certainly an exaggeration, Hancock's prompt action in guarding his stores from secessionist mobs saved the army a great deal of trouble in the ensuing months.

In the first few days of war, all of California was seething with fears and rumors—most of them exaggerations, as events later proved. A charge was made that Brigadier General Albert Sidney Johnston, commander of the U. S. Army's Department of the Pacific since January 1861, was plotting to turn the state over to the Confederacy. Johnston, a Kentuckian by birth and an officer highly respected by his cohorts, was certainly torn by conflicting loyalties but there is not a shred of evidence implicating him in any conspiracy.

[2] Maymie R. Krythe, "First Hotel in Old Los Angeles: The Romantic Bella Union," *H.S.S.C. Quarterly*, June 1951. See also Newmark, p. 294; and *Star*, May 4 and 11, 1861.
[3] Hancock, pp. 59–60; and Glen Tucker, *Hancock The Superb* (Indianapolis: Bobbs-Merrill Co., 1960), pp. 62–63.
[4] Tucker, p. 62.

Nevertheless, the rumor reached Lincoln's ears and Brigadier General Edwin Sumner was sent west to replace him. Johnston tendered his resignation from the army on April 9th, two weeks before Sumner's arrival. He remained at his post, however, until relieved by General Sumner on April 25th.[5]

While awaiting replacement in San Francisco, Johnston agonized over his future. He was nearing sixty, and had a wife and five children to support. His wife was the sister of Dr. John S. Griffin of Los Angeles. At Griffin's invitation, Johnston decided to settle in Los Angeles and, he hoped at the time, accept any civilian employment that would support his family. A few days after turning over his command to General Sumner, Johnston was on his way south on the steamer *Senator*, reaching San Pedro on May 6th. For more than a month, he lived with his brother-in-law in Los Angeles, increasingly restless and torn between the desire to live here and the urge to help his native South.[6]

General Sumner, new commander of the Department of the Pacific in San Francisco, made a quick survey of the war situation in California and was distressed with what he found. In his first report to Washington, sent the day after his arrival, he painted a grim picture: "There is a strong Union feeling with the majority of the people of this state, but the secessionists are much the most active and zealous party, which gives them more influence than they ought to have from their numbers. I have no doubt there is some deep scheming to draw California into the secession movement— in the first place as the 'Republic of the Pacific,' expecting afterwards to induce her to join the Southern Confederacy."[7] On April 30th, Sumner narrowed his sights on southern Cali-

[5] Aurora Hunt, *The Army of the Pacific, 1860–1866* (Glendale: Arthur H. Clark Co., 1951), p. 21.
[6] Avery C. Moore, *Destiny's Soldier* (San Francisco: Fearon Publishers, 1958), pp. 39–40, 53: and Charles P. Roland, *Albert Sidney Johnston: Soldier of Three Republics* (Austin: University of Texas Press, 1964), pp. 250–252.
[7] *O.R.*, Ser. I, Vol. L, Part 1, p. 462.

Winfield Scott Hancock

Albert Johnston

Henry D. Barrows

General George Wright

fornia: "I have found it necessary to withdraw the troops from Fort Mojave and place them at Los Angeles. There is more danger of disaffection at this place than any other in the state. There are a number of influential men there who are decided Secessionists, and if we have difficulty it will commence there."[8] Three days later, the General ordered Company K, 1st Dragoons, to proceed immediately from Fort Tejon to Los Angeles.[9] And not a moment too soon.

That a display of force was urgently needed in Los Angeles to counter secessionist threats was clearly revealed in letters Captain Hancock sent General Sumner during early May. On May 4th, Hancock indicated that the situation in Los Angeles was critical but that he might be able to muster sufficient loyal citizens to counter an expected attack from "a number of reckless people who have nothing to lose." He wrote that the secessionists had possession of "a new bronze fieldpiece and carriage (I think a 6-pounder gun)," and that "it might be wise to send here a gun of equal or greater caliber." Later he added that "a 12-pounder howitzer . . . would be best (two might be better)."[10] Three days later, Hancock reported, "The 'bear flag' was paraded through the streets of El Monte (twelve miles eastward) on the 4th instant, and was escorted by a number of horsemen, varying (according to reports) from forty to seventy, most probably the former. . . . The 'bear flag' is being painted here, and I think it will be paraded soon, possibly next Sunday, or some other day when the company known as the secession company drills. I have taken all the precautions possible and that I think necessary, and I believe I can get all the assistance I require until the troops arrive, from among the citizens, to resist any open attack upon the public property." Hancock further stated that the dragoons with artillery would have "a strong moral ef-

[8] *Ibid.*, p. 474.
[9] *Ibid.*, p. 475.
[10] *Ibid.*, p. 476.

fect" on the rebelling populace, and urged that "a show be made at once." Not only was Hancock concerned about secessionists among the Anglo elements, he was increasingly worried about discontent among Los Angeles' Spanish-speaking citizens: "When once a revolution commences the masses of the native population will act, and they are worthy of a good deal of consideration. If they act it will be most likely against the Government." [11]

Los Angeles narrowly averted bloodshed a few days later. A company of fifty or sixty mounted secessionists from El Monte—probably the same ones who raised the Bear Flag in that Southern-sympathizing community—planned to ride into Los Angeles and raise the Bear Flag, symbol of resistance to the federal government, over the Court House. Union men in Los Angeles got wind of this plan and went to Sheriff Tomás Sánchez, warning him that such an attempt would be forceably resisted and that bloodshed might develop. Sánchez, although himself sympathetic to the Confederate cause, had the good sense to realize that such a confrontation would have dire consequences. The sheriff, at the last minute, sent a messenger to El Monte to ask the Bear Flaggers to abandon, or at least delay, their plan. The messenger intercepted the mounted "Monte Boys" already enroute to Los Angeles and handed them the sheriff's request, along with a warning that fighting would ensue if they proceeded into Los Angeles. With reluctance, the Monte Boys turned around and went home. [12]

On May 14th, Major James Henry Carleton and fifty mounted troopers of Company K, 1st Dragoons, from Fort Tejon, trotted into Los Angeles, to the immense relief of Captain Hancock and Union sympathizers in town. A few days later they were joined by cavalry units from Fort Mojave, and the immediate danger of an armed insurrection in Los

[11] *Ibid.*, p. 480.
[12] Arthur Woodward, "Confederate Secret Societies in California," *The Westerners Brand Book, Los Angeles Corral*, 1949.

BY-LAWS

OF

𝕷𝖔𝖘 𝕬𝖓𝖌𝖊𝖑𝖊𝖘 𝕮𝖔𝖚𝖓𝖈𝖎𝖑,

NO. 85, U. L. A.

LOS ANGELES,

Los Angeles County, California.

Adopted, June 29, 1863.

CONW.·   ·TE, PRINTERS.

Union Forever! Badge, Los Angeles, May 25, 1861

Angeles was over. The soldiers set up camp on the southern outskirts of town, in line-of-sight with Captain Hancock's Quartermaster building, in case the latter might need help. The new encampment was named Camp Fitzgerald in honor of Major E. F. Fitzgerald, late of Fort Tejon, who had died a year earlier.[13] Its location was at the base of the hill between 1st and 2nd Streets, on Fort Street (later Broadway), and it initially consisted of eleven tents in a cleared area 100 yards wide and 150 yards long.[14]

With soldiers in blue patroling the streets of Los Angeles, citizens loyal to the Union were finally able to express themselves. A Union Club was organized; Columbus Sims was elected president and J. J. Warner vice president. The club passed a resolution stating, in part, "We, the citizens of Los Angeles, declare our devotion to the Union and to the Government; sustain and support the Constitution; and will to the extent of our lives and means resist treasonable spirit."[15]

Los Angeles Unionists, with the support of Major Carleton and his 1st Dragoons, boldly made plans for a "Grand Union Demonstration" to be held May 25th. There would be a parade and speeches, climaxed by the hoisting of the Stars and Stripes over the Court House. This was a direct challenge to the secessionist majority. A few days before the demonstration, a warning was posted in front of the Bella Union that anyone raising the national flag over the Court House would be shot dead. And on the morning of May 25th, a rumor circulated that a party of armed secessionists would physically prevent the flag raising. But neither of these intimidations came to pass. At the prescribed time, Union men from as far away as New San Pedro, guarded by armed dragoons in full dress, gathered in the Plaza. The 1st Dragoon band struck up a march and the procession of civilians and soldiers proceeded

[13] Helen S. Giffen and Arthur Woodward, *The Story of El Tejon* (Los Angeles: Dawson's Book Shop, 1942), p. 121.
[14] *Star*, June 8, 1861; Giffen and Woodward, p. 121.
[15] *Southern News*, May 15, 1861.

to the Court House. Phineas Banning mounted the steps, gave a short but rousing speech, and presented a large national flag to Columbus Sims, president of the Union Club. Patriotic orations by Major Carleton, Captain Hancock, and Ezra Drown followed. The dragoons, "with their glistening sabers and burnished carbines," added to the dignity of the occasion. To a hushed audience, the Stars and Stripes was slowly hoisted high over the building, the first time the flag had flown over Los Angeles since the news of Fort Sumter. The demonstration concluded with a salute of 34 guns—one for each state in the Union—and a round of rousing cheers. Only one incident marred the occasion: an over-zealous Union supporter attempted to read a patriotic poem from an upstairs window in the Bella Union and was promptly pitched into the street by Rebel sympathizers.[16]

Early in June, more troops reached Los Angeles. Fort Tejon was all but abandoned as the remaining company of the 1st Dragoons moved to Camp Fitzgerald. Two companies of the 6th Infantry Regiment marched in from Fort Mojave and San Diego. Camp Fitzgerald was relocated two miles south of town, along San Pedro Road, to accomodate the enlarged troop complement and provide better pasture for the horses.[17] Los Angeles became a garrison town, with soldiers in blue patroling the streets during the daytime to the stares of a largely hostile populace.

When Fort Tejon was abandoned, Lieutenant Edward F. Beale's famous Camel Corps was moved to Los Angeles. On June 14th, citizens lined the streets in amused awe as the strange procession of 31 ungainly beasts entered town. The camels were at first corraled behind Captain Hancock's Quar-

---

[16] *Southern News*, May 29, 1861; *Star*, June 1, 1861; Newmark, p. 296; Maymie Krythe, *Port Admiral: Phineas Banning, 1830–1885* (San Francisco: California Historical Society, 1957), pp. 106–107; and Aurora Hunt, *Major General James Henry Carleton, Western Frontier Dragoon* (Glendale: Arthur H. Clark Co., 1958), pp. 187–191.

[17] *Star*, June 8, 1861; and Hunt, *Army of the Pacific*, p. 42.

California Volunteers drilling in San Francisco, 1862

Washington Square, San Francisco, July 4, 1862

termaster Headquarters on Main Street near 3rd, much to the delight of neighborhood children and the annoyance of older residents. In October, they were moved to another corral at the corner of 2nd and Spring streets, next to the brick school house. For several months, until moved to Camp Drum near Wilmington, the obnoxious and ill-tempered creatures were a common sight about town.[18]

While loyal army officers in Los Angeles, by order of General Sumner, were taking an oath of allegiance to the United States in the Court House,[19] other officers, recently resigned because of sympathy with the Southern cause, were hiding out in town. Among them were names that soon were to become famous—Albert Sidney Johnston, George Pickett, Lewis Armistead, Richard Garnett.[20] Their immediate problem was how to reach Richmond, Virginia, to offer their services to the Confederacy. When the opportunity arose, they would devise a plan.

[18] *Star*, June 22, 1861; Giffen and Woodward, pp. 89–90.
[19] *Star*, June 15, 1861.
[20] Tucker, pp. 61–63; Roland, pp. 252–254.

SUMMER OF UNREST

ALBERT SIDNEY JOHNSTON, lately brigadier general, United States Army, had every reason to stay in Los Angeles. His brother-in-law, Dr. John S. Griffin, was a splendid host, his wife Eliza was with child, and he himself was of an age when most men think of retirement. But his native South was fighting for her life, and his sense of honor, ingrained from a lifetime of military service, would not allow him to stand aside. He must offer his services to the Confederacy in its great hour of need.

After eliciting a vow from Dr. Griffin that he would care for Eliza and the children, Johnston began thinking of an escape to the Confederacy. His first plan was to take ship to Panama, cross the Isthmus, and continue by sea to New York, then south to Richmond. But he received word that his arrest had been ordered by the Secretary of War, and this avenue of escape was closed. A few days later Johnston learned from friends that a Captain Alonzo Ridley was secretly organizing a party of former military officers and secession-minded civilians for an overland march to Texas. He at once joined the group. The party's departure from Los Angeles was first set for June 22nd, but a rumor was circulated that the date was known to federal authorities so it was secretly moved up to June 16th.[1]

---

[1] Roland, pp. 251–252; Moore, pp. 53–54.

The evening before departure, Johnston and five other former army officers who had opted to cast their lot with the
Confederacy were invited to dinner at the home of Captain
and Mrs. Hancock. Hancock and all those assembled for the
occasion were close friends, having served together in the 6th
Infantry many years. Although Hancock was not directly
informed of the group's imminent escape, he must have suspected their plans. It was a mournful gathering. "All were
endeavoring to conceal, under smiling exteriors, hearts that
were filled with sadness over the sundering of life-long ties."[2]
Most disconsolate was Major Lewis Armistead who, with
tears streaming down his face, presented his new major's
uniform to Hancock, then turned to Mrs. Hancock and handed her a small satchel of personal belongings, requesting that
they be sent to his family in the event of his death. An emotional farewell ended the gathering.[3]

Less than a year later, Albert Sidney Johnston would die
commanding the Confederate army at Shiloh. Four of the
other five Confederate officers present that night at Captain
Hancock's Los Angeles home would, two years later, face
Hancock again, by this time Major General Hancock, commander of the Union Army's II Corps at Gettysburg. Three
of them—Lewis Armistead leading Pickett's famous charge,
Richard Garnett, and one other whose name is not now
known—would die within a few hundred feet of Hancock's
command post on Cemetery Ridge. Only George Pickett, also
present at that farewell dinner, would remain alive, but
would forever relive the agony of watching his splendid
troops cut to pieces by soldiers of Hancock's army corps.[4] How
strange and ironic the fortunes of war!

It was agreed, to lessen the chances of detection, that those
escaping with Captain Ridley would leave Los Angeles sepa-

[2] Hancock, p. 69.
[3] Ibid., pp. 69–70; Tucker, pp. 64–65.
[4] Tucker, p. 65.

rately and rendezvous near Warner's Ranch, 100 miles to the southeast. One by one, at different times and taking different routes, the Confederacy-bound volunteers stole out of town. General Johnston departed before dawn on June 16th, on horseback, with provisions in a light ambulance wagon pulled by two mules, and accompanied only by his trusted Negro servant Rand and a secessionist guide named Freeze. The small party rested at Chino Ranch for a few hours, then continued via the old Butterfield route to the rendezvous. Several days later the entire party, eight former 6th Infantry Regiment officers and 25 civilians, assembled at Warner's Ranch, and on June 29th started out on their gruelling desert march.

Even today, a mid-summer trip from Warner's Ranch across the Anza-Borrego desert and Imperial Valley to Yuma is a hot and rather unpleasant trip. In 1861 it was a brutal test of human endurance over scorching rock and sand with almost no water enroute. The small band of secessionists suffered greatly from stifling heat and thirst, but after a six-day toil, traveling mostly in the early morning and evening hours, reached the Colorado River a few miles north of Fort Yuma. Upon discovering that the fort was garrisoned by only a small army unit, several of the more rabid secessionists wanted to seize and burn it, but were dissuaded from doing so by General Johnston.[5] The remainder of the journey through Arizona, the narrow escape from capture near Dragoon Springs, Arizona, and the encounter with hostile Apaches are beyond the scope of this book; suffice to say that Johnston and his fellow officers made it safely to Richmond and joined the Confederate Army.

In Los Angeles, the 4th of July, 1861, was observed in a subdued manner. Citizens loyal to the Union and soldiers assembled in the Plaza for a patriotic speech by Captain

---

[5] Johnston's journey from Los Angeles to the Confederacy is covered in Moore, pp. 54–55; Roland, pp. 252–256; and William Preston Johnston, *The Life of General Albert Sidney Johnston* (New York: D. Appleton & Co., 1878), pp. 275–291.

Hancock, then marched southeast to the shady grove of Don
Luís Sainsevain for more speeches and a picnic.[6]

Camp Fitzgerald was moved twice within a month: first
to a site two miles south of Los Angeles, then two weeks later
to "a large plain" three-fourths of a mile south of town.[7] Here
there was sufficient space for the four companies assigned to
Los Angeles—B and K of the 1st Dragoons, F and I of the 6th
Infantry—and pasturage for the horses. Major James Henry
Carleton was making a show of force to impress—or intimi-
date—the local populace. The soldiers drilled constantly and
were in a high state of discipline. There was inspection and
dress parade every Sunday morning at 9 a.m. On July 28th,
the citizens of Los Angeles were invited to watch a sham battle.
The *Star* described it: "The infantry were all out in the
plains south of the camp, deployed as skirmishers. . . . The
cavalry, under command of Captain Davidson, bore down
upon the line of skirmishers at full gallop, giving a shout as
they came near, using carbines (with blank cartridges, of
course), and sabres as they closed upon the line. . . . When
the two lines met, the smoke and shouting, with the sharp
crack of arms, seemed dangerously thrilling, and we were
glad to hear that the casualties only amounted to three or
four hats knocked off and a couple of kits scattered." Afterwards there was a full dress parade, witnessed by a large
crowd from town.[8]

In August 1861, two pieces of news reached Los Angeles
that gave a tremendous lift to secessionist spirits and almost
overnight renewed the crisis atmosphere, not only in the
city, but all over southern California.

Dispatches from Virginia and Washington, telling of the
Union Army's crushing defeat at Bull Run, were printed on
the front pages of both the *Star* and the *Southern News*. The

[6] *Star*, July 6, 1861; Newmark, p. 300.
[7] *Ibid.*, July 13, 1861.
[8] *Ibid.*, August 3, 1861.

Southern News, now an outright Unionist paper after several months of fence straddling, reported that secessionists in town were delighted and celebrating in the streets.[9] The *Star* could not hide its elation, and in a lengthy editorial, blamed the Union defeat on Lincoln and the "New York abolition press" that allegedly had forced General Winfield Scott's hand.[10]

Equally damaging to the Union cause, in the eyes of local secessionists, was the Confederate invasion of New Mexico that began on July 23, 1861, when Lieutenant Colonel John R. Baylor marched forty miles up the Rio Grande and captured Mesilla. On August 1st, Baylor proclaimed the Confederate Territory of Arizona—all of New Mexico and Arizona south of the 34th parallel, stretching from Texas to California—and appointed himself governor. About the same time, the United States Army abandoned all of its forts in southern Arizona, and it appeared evident, at least to those with Confederate sympathies, that the occupation of the territory by the C.S.A. was imminent. Baylor himself had his eyes on California, and wrote to his superior, a short time later, that California was on the "eve of revolution." [11]

The rumors that accompanied the news of Confederate successes were alarming. There were fears that secessionists were about to seize Lower California and make it a base for operations on the Pacific Coast, that a Confederate force was on the way to Guaymas to seize the Mexican seaport, that Confederate cruisers were already operating in Pacific waters.[12]

The apparent upturn in Southern fortunes was jubilantly celebrated in Los Angeles, and "Secesh" sympathizers rode through the streets howling for Jeff Davis and the Confeder-

[9] *Southern News*, August 14, 1861.
[10] *Star*, August 10, 17 and 24, 1861.
[11] Ray C. Colton, *The Civil War in the Western Territories* (Norman: University of Oklahoma Press, 1959), pp. 13–19, 200; W. H. Watford, "The Far-Western Wing of the Rebelloin," *C.H.S. Quarterly*, June 1955.
[12] Beattie, p. 362.

acy's newest hero, Stonewall Jackson. Soldiers in blue were treated with such contempt at the Bella Union that the hotel was placed off limits to army personnel.[13] A correspondent of the *San Francisco Journal* spent a night at the Main Street hostelry and described it as "the most noted Secessionist rendezvous in the whole city. . . . I have proposed to the landlord to call it the 'Belly Union,' as most of the patrons get pot-gutted the moment an expression of sympathy is made for Uncle Sam. All my surroundings are 'Dixies.' Dogs bark it, asses and mules bray it, and bilious bipeds whistle it. The whole air is full of it. . . . I am not going to get myself in any more messes by endeavoring to prove to these semi-insane people that to hoist the Stars and Stripes is not a treason against Secession."[14]

Abel Stearns, lately turned Republican and staunchly loyal to the Union, wrote to General Sumner on August 9th, and again on the 10th, requesting that two more companies of troops be sent here to insure southern California against insurrection. Stearns was particularly concerned about native Californians in the community, stating that there exist here "a class of persons who are endeavoring to work this element into shape for evil purposes." He was also worried about disunion sentiments in San Bernardino and Holcomb Valley, where "a nearly complete organization exists."[15]

"I wish to God the Union men would hold up their heads more here," wrote Captain John W. Davidson, temporarily in command at Camp Fitzgerald while Major Carleton was in San Francisco. Davidson proposed the formation of a Los Angeles Home Guard, made up of 100 or more local citizens of unquestionable loyalty to the Union.[16] The plan was accepted by General Sumner, and the Los Angeles Home Guard was organized on August 13th. A. B. Hayward was elected

13 Krythe, "Bella Union," p. 163.
14 *Ibid.*, p. 164.
15 *O.R.*, Ser. I, Vol. L, Part 1, pp. 563–565.
16 *Ibid.*, pp. 562–563.

chairman, and among the members sworn to keep Los Angeles safe for the Union were such prominent citizens as Abel Stearns, F. P. F. Temple, J. J. Warner, Ezra Drown, Henry D. Barrows, and the Negro ex-slave Robert Owens.[17] The army ordnance officer at Benicia Arsenal shipped down 150 muskets with 6,000 rounds of ball ammunition for the volunteer guards. The *Star* called them "Uncle Abe's right Arm" who pledged themselves to "keep Dixie straight in this quarter."[18]

The problem of garrisoning secession-minded southern California while at the same time sending regular army officers east to the war theater, as ordered by the Secretary of War Simon Cameron, perplexed General Sumner. To serve this dual purpose, Congress passed the Volunteer Employment Act of July 19, 1861, requesting each state to supply military volunteers to guard the home front while the regulars went to war. Cameron telegraphed Governor Downey that the California quota under this act was one regiment of infantry and five companies of cavalry. In August, to meet the Confederate invasion threat, Cameron increased the state quota by four additional regiments of infantry and one of cavalry.[19] But it would be several months before these volunteers would be ready for duty. Meanwhile, General Sumner received repeated warnings that the southern part of the state was in dire peril. He felt he had no choice but to increase the number of troops in this region and delay their shipment east. Late in August, two more companies, D and K of the 4th Infantry, arrived in New San Pedro and were hurried to Camp Fitzgerald.[20] Sumner justified his action in a dispatch to the War Department in September: "The disaffection in the southern part of the state is increasing and becoming dangerous, and it is indispensably necessary to throw reenforcements into that section immediately. The rebels are organizing, collect-

[17] *Ibid.*, pp. 568–569.
[18] *Star*, August 31, 1861.
[19] Hunt, *Carleton*, p. 194.
[20] *Star*, August 24 and 31, 1861.

ing supplies, and evidently preparing to receive a force from Texas, and the worst feature of the affair is this: they have managed to seduce the native Californians by telling them they will be ruined by taxes to maintain the war." [21]

General Sumner was undoubtedly referring to the *Star's* violent outburst against the war tax measure enacted by Congress in August. Hamilton charged that the tax was "to enable the Administration to carry on a wholesale butchery of the people of the Southern States, who have the temerity to ask to be let alone, and allowed to govern themselves." He then raged about how the tax would affect local citizens: "Freemen! Read the foregoing section of the late Act of Congress, imposing a direct tax. Under it the Assessor, appointed by Mr. Lincoln, has the right to enter your house, to examine your wife's bedchamber, to open the drawers of your bureau, to go into your kitchen, to seize the key to your safe and open it and count your money, to take your book of accounts, your ledger, and extract the sum to tax you. . . . Great God! Was ever such a law devised? Woe to you who do not support 'Uncle Abe,' for he is invested with greater power than ever Caesar possessed over the Romans." Hamilton ended his protest with a bit of sarcastic humor: "His Imperial Majesty, Abraham the Second (in direct succession from the illustrious Founder of the Kings of the Earth), Emperor of the United Sovereignties of America, has been graciously pleased to order that a tax of 15 cents a pound be levied upon all tea, coffee and sugar consumed by his subjects—for the purpose of subduing his enemies." [22]

Hamilton's crusade against the war tax apparently was successful in creating unrest among the Spanish-speaking citizenry. Captain Davidson did his utmost to counter the *Star's* claims and show the Californians that the federal government was their friend. He reported to headquarters,

[21] *O.R.*, Ser. I, Vol. L., Pt. 1, p. 623.
[22] *Star*, August 31, 1861.

Department of the Pacific, what measures he had taken: "Arrangements have been made with the Catholic bishop of this diocese to hold divine service in camp every alternate Sunday. This will have effect with the native Californians and show them that they and the troops have a common sympathy upon this ground. The vicar-general (Father Raho) assures me . . . that the greater portion of the Californians are friendly to the Government, and that the ideas to the contrary which have been entertained about those of this county are groundless." [23]

Los Angeles lost its best known army officer the last week of August when Captain Winfield Scott Hancock, quartermaster here for more than two years, set sail for the eastern war zone and eventual fame. Before he boarded, Phineas Banning, in appreciation of Captain Hancock's services, christened his new little harbor steamer the *Ada Hancock*, in honor of the Captain's five-year-old daughter.[24]

Politics once again became a topic of local interest with the September elections just around the corner. The main interest was in the three-way race for governor among Leland Stanford, Republican; John Conness, Union Democrat; and John McConnell, Regular Democrat. A "People's Union Convention" was held at the Court House on August 5th, attended by Douglas Democrats and Republicans, to select candidates for state and local offices. The ticket of the local branch of the People's Union Party was headed by Abel Stearns, candidate for the state senate. All candidates chosen were "unconditional supporters of our great and glorious National Government." [25]

The Democrats assembled at the Court House two weeks later and quickly demonstrated their secessionist feelings: "Resolved, that we look upon the present war waged by President Lincoln as an abolition war, waged for abolition pur-

[23] *O.R.*, Ser. I., Vol. L, Pt. 1, p. 582.
[24] Hancock, p. 71.
[25] *Southern News*, August 7, 1861.

poses, and that in its unholy pursuit the Constitution of our country has been overthrown in a blind and fanatical admiration of the negro."[26] McConnell was supported for governor, and Colonel J. R. Vineyard was nominated for the state senate.

On election day, September 4th, the *Southern News* urged Los Angeles voters to support the Union: "Today's issue will decide whether our State is to be given into the hands of the disunionists, or whether a true and loyal man shall guide the destinies of our young, peaceful and prosperous state. We conjure every man who loves the great and glorious Government . . . to vote against the secession ticket, both state and county."[27]

That Los Angeles County was still strongly secession-minded was demonstrated loud and clear by the election returns. Although California as a whole went Unionist, and Leland Stanford became the first Republican governor in the state's history, in this county the anti-Union candidates won by a wide margin:[28]

For Governor	Los Angeles City	Los Angeles County
McConnell (Democrat)	578	1187
Conness (Union Democrat)	96	216
Stanford Republican)	195	455

Colonel Vineyard routed Abel Stearns for state senator by a vote of 583 to 265, and Regular Democrats were likewise victorious in every local contest.

The *Star*, as expected, was overjoyed: "Never in this county has the Democratic party been so nobly sustained."[29]

The *Southern News* expressed the feelings of shock and chagrin of the Union minority in town: "The Union party has been utterly defeated in this county. Secession and dis-

---

26 *Star*, August 24. 1861.
27 *Southern News*, September 4, 1861.
28 *Star*, September 7, 1861.
29 *Ibid.*

union have carried the day, and years of repentence cannot wash out the stain. Abroad we shall be set down as a county not to be relied upon; and as a county containing naught but traitors and conspirators against the Government."[30]

The *Southern News* apparently suffered hard times because of its Union position in a strongly secessionist town. The El Monte deputy postmaster, A. J. Hern, was a secessionist and refused to deliver the newspaper to local subscribers.[31] Most of the Jewish population in Los Angeles cancelled their subscriptions in protest after the *News* criticized them for voting the secession ticket. Among those cancelling were the mayor, Damien Marchessault, and businessmen Harris Newmark and Charles Ducommun. The *News* defiantly asserted, "As long as we control this paper, it shall never contain anything that is disloyal. . . . Though we should be left without one solitary subscriber, this paper will boldly declaim against the Tories, and nail at its mast-head the Flag of our Union."[32]

[30] *Southern News*, September 6, 1861.
[31] *Ibid.*, August 16, 1861.
[32] *Ibid.*, September 11, 1861.

CONSPIRACY: REAL OR IMAGINED

THE CONFEDERATE INVASION of Arizona stirred Los Angeles and caused near panic among Unionists. In early September, the *Star* reported—prematurely as it turned out—that Confederate troops had reached the village of Picacho, 40 miles northwest of Tuscon.[1] Rumors of a rebel army nearing the Colorado River, 14,000 Texas troops poised along the Sonora border, and Arizona lost to the Union occupied the *Southern News*: "Everything in that quarter [Arizona] is now under the control of secessionists, who are making rapid strides toward the Pacific coast, where they are yet determined to gain a foothold."[2] The fact that most of these stories were gross exaggerations made no difference; people read and believed them, and reacted accordingly.

The center of secessionist activity in southern California, in the fall of 1861, appeared to be San Bernardino and Holcomb Valley, in the mountains to the north. As early as June 3rd, Edwin A. Sherman, Unionist editor of the *San Bernardino Patriot*, wrote to General Sumner that "Secret meetings continue to be held all over this lower country, and secession and disunion are boldly avowed in our streets. Shooting continues to be the order of the day, and drunken desperadoes and Southern cutthroats damn the Stars and Stripes and en-

[1] *Star*, September 7, 1861.
[2] *Southern News*, September 27, 1861.

[73]

deavor to create disturbances most of the time."[3] In July Sumner dispatched Major Carleton from Los Angeles to San Bernardino to investigate the situation there. Carleton's report, while not supporting Sherman's extreme claims, did recommend that two or more companies of soldiers be stationed there.[4] Accordingly, Major William S. Ketchum was ordered to San Bernardino with four companies of infantry on August 13th. Within a few days Ketchum and two of the four companies were encamped just south of town. Rumors that his infantry units were about to be assaulted by secessionists caused Ketchum to send an urgent request to Captain Davidson, asking that two companies of dragoons from Los Angeles be dispatched immediately as reenforcements.[5] But no attack occurred, and by the end of the month San Bernardino was considered under control.

The situation in Holcomb Valley, a gold mining camp high in the San Bernardino Mountains, appeared to be much more serious. The mountain valley was alleged to contain hundreds, even thousands, of Confederate sympathizers, only posing as miners, and to be a recruitment center and rendezvous for volunteers destined for the Southern army.[6] The *Southern News* went so far as to claim that 200 armed secessionists from Holcomb Valley were planning a march on Los Angeles to seize government stores.[7]

The rumors reached epic proportions by the time they reached San Francisco. The *Alta California* reported 2,000 armed secessionists in Los Angeles and San Bernardino counties, completely organized, controlled by secret organizations, and ready to rendezvous anywhere their leaders directed.[8]

[3] *O.R.*, Ser. I, Vol. L, Pt. 1, p. 497.
[4] *O.R.*, Ser. I, Vol. L, Pt. 1, pp. 548–551.
[5] *Ibid.*, pp. 567, 585, 594; and Beattie, pp. 373–374.
[6] Beattie, p. 367.
[7] *Southern News*, August 21, 1861.
[8] *Alta California*, September 9, 1861.

What secret organizations? The two main ones in California were the Knights of the Columbian Star and the Knights of the Golden Circle, both avowed supporters of the Confederate cause. Being undercover groups, they went unmentioned in the contemporary press, but, thanks to Union informers and detectives employed by the army to infiltrate the organizations, the federal authorities were fairly well posted concerning their activities.

The Knights of the Columbian Star were apparently strongest in the San Francisco area, as few of their activities in southern California have come to light. The society was cloaked in such secrecy that few members were aware of the entirety of the organization. It was divided into three divisions, or "degrees," each with its own signs, passwords, and grips. The "governor-general" of the Knights of the Columbian Star was believed to be Beriah Brown, editor of the San Francisco *Democratic Press*.[9]

Much more active in Los Angeles and San Bernardino counties were the Knights of the Golden Circle. This secret secessionist society has been described as extremely well organized, with a membership numbering in thousands, with leaders who were "bold, daring, talented men of indomitable will and courage, who exercised an unlimited control over their followers."[10] They also were well armed and took oaths of secrecy complete with special passwords and handshakes. Clarence Bennett of San Bernardino, through a friend in Holcomb Valley who posed as a secessionist, secured a copy of their pledge and constitution, which he forwarded to General Sumner in San Francisco. Along with resolutions in support of the Constitution and against the Lincoln administration. the Knights of the Golden Circle resolved that "we are in

[9] Benjamin Franklin Gilbert, "The Confederate Minority in California," *C.H.S. Quarterly*, June 1941, pp. 155–156.
[10] Imogene Spaulding, "The Attitude of California to the Civil War," *Annual Publications of the H.S.S.C.*, 1912–1913, p. 112.

favor of sustaining the southern states of the American Confederacy in all their constitutional rights; that we believe an unconstitutional war is now being waged against them to subject them to a taxation enormous and unequal and to deprive them in the end of their species of property called slaves. The members resolved to "mutually pledge to each other our lives, our property, and our sacred honor to sustain our brethren of the southern states in the just defense of their constitutional rights." Then each Knight signed an oath to uphold the secrecy of the organization and obey instructions: "All this I solemnly swear to obey under penalty of being shot."[11]

The main efforts of the Knights of the Golden Circle were apparently directed at recruiting for the Confederate army and helping these volunteers get to the Confederacy. It was common for the recruits to pose as miners enroute to gold diggings on the Colorado River. Although a host of rumors had them ready to begin an insurrection in southern California, the Knights never actually struck a blow for the Confederacy. However, if Confederate forces in Arizona had ever reached the Colorado River, an armed revolt here may well have occurred; General Sumner thought this a strong possibility.[12] "Tooch" Martin, a member of the Knights of the Golden Circle, El Monte Lodge, interviewed in 1924, claimed that "if the Confederacy had captured Washington we would have struck a blow here."[13]

The size and strength of the Knights of the Golden Circle have never been ascertained. Estimates run as high as 100,000 for the state as a whole, but this is most certainly a gross

---

[11] O.R., Ser. I, Vol. L, Pt. 1, pp. 556–558. The Knights of the Golden Circle was an old organization in the South, dating back into the 1830s. For their history, see Leonard B. Waitman, "The Knights of the Golden Circle," San Bernardino County Museum Association Quarterly, Summer 1968.

[12] O.R., Ser. I, Vol. L, Pt. 1, p. 610.

[13] Percival J. Cooney, "Southern California in Civil War Days," Annual Publications, H.S.S.C. 1924, p. 59.

exaggeration.[14] A more accurate guess would be around 16,000.[15] In southern California, with its large secessionist population, the proportion of members was most likely higher than in the northern part of the state. Tooch Martin remembered a big lodge of Knights in El Monte, "almost everyone belonging to it except the three or four living down on what was known as 'Black Republican Alley'—the Durfees, the Johnsons and a few others."[16]

The most detailed report of the Knights of the Golden Circle activities in southern California was made by Gustav Brown, a federal detective who claimed to have infiltrated the organization in 1864. Brown claimed that the Knights had 253 secret members in Los Angeles County, of whom 54 lived in Los Angeles city, 92 resided in El Monte, and 27 worked in the San Gabriel Canyon mines. The "Governor" of the Los Angeles County Knights was alleged to be Charles Howard and the "Lieutenant Governor" J. M. Callan, both residents of Los Angeles. Detective Brown further stated that the local Knights of the Golden Circle had a secret rendezvous on Rock Creek in the San Gabriel Mountains. Writing of this hidden hideout, Brown described it as follows: "It is in the mountains, and has plenty of wood, water and grass. There are but four or five there now herding cattle. They intend to unite at this place in case of a draft being ordered and commence guerrilla warfare."[17]

How much of a threat to Union control of California were these secret organizations? This question has long been argued by historians. Some saw a dangerous, widespread conspiracy that narrowly missed delivering the state to the Confederacy. But most historians today would probably agree with Benjamin Franklin Gilbert that "Although their size

[14] Charles Mial Dustin, "The Knights of the Golden Circle," *Pacific Monthly*, November 1911.

[15] Gilbert, p. 154.

[16] Cooney, p. 59.

[17] Woodward, "Confederate Secret Societies in California"; Spaulding, p. 114.

and strength were exaggerated by alarmists, the Confederate were never organized to the degree of offering real resistance to Union control."[18] Still, had the Confederate Army from Texas ever reached and crossed the Colorado River, the Knights of the Golden Circle might well have acted. Of course, one today can only speculate about the outcome.

In September 1861, Captain Davidson and a company of the 1st Dragoons left Camp Fitzgerald for San Bernardino, once again a trouble spot because of hotly-contested elections. When Davidson went into town, he was rudely greeted with shouts of "Hurrah for Jeff Davis! Hurrah for the Southern Confederacy!" One slightly inebriated secessionist yelled, "If the Union men think they can whip us, let them come on —we can out-fight them, out-steal them, out-murder them and out-vote them."[19] Captain Davidson then left town and returned a short time later with his dragoons, threatening arrest to anyone voicing disloyal sentiments. In the face of the loaded rifles and drawn swords of the mounted soldiers, no one did.[20]

In Los Angeles, Henry D. Barrows, U. S. Marshal for the Southern District, was writing weekly reports for the *San Francisco Bulletin*. On September 26th he reported, "The United States Hotel here, which was tabooed by Captain Davidson on account of Secession influence, and an order issued that no soldier at this point should enter it, nor the Bella Union either, under penalty of court-martial, has

---

[18] Gilbert, p. 154; see also Peter Heywood Wang, "The Mythical Confederate Plot in Southern California," *San Bernardino County Museum Association Quarterly*, Summer 1969. Wang makes a credible point that historians have failed to to differentiate between pro-Southern and anti-Lincoln administration sentiment in southern California. Many local citizens, while not particularly Confederate sympathizers, were strongly at odds with the federal government. The Spanish-speaking native Californians would fit in this category. "My enemy's enemy is my friend" was not necessarily true in California of the 1860s.

[19] *Star*, September 14, 1861.

[20] *Ibid*.

changed hands, and is now kept by a good Union German, and the Stars and Stripes raised over it, and the order withdrawn." [21]

During late September and October, 1861, southern California was a beehive of troop movements. The California Volunteers, conscripted since July to replace army regulars, began arriving in force. They were transported from San Francisco south to New San Pedro on the wooden steamers *Oregon*, *Senator*, *Pacific*, and on the naval vessels *Shubrick* and *Active*. The first contingent, seven companies of the 1st Infantry Regiment, reached Phineas Banning's port on September 18th. [22] Next day they were marched to a new camp along Ballona Creek (today's Culver City), about eight miles southwest of Los Angeles. The camp soon was named Camp Latham, after Milton S. Latham, former California governor (for five days) and later senator. [23]

California volunteers continued to reach New San Pedro almost daily, and by October 6th there were over 1,200 men undergoing rigorous training at Camp Latham. The first post commander was Colonel Joseph R. West, but he was soon succeeded by Colonel George Washington Bowie, "a fine looking portly gentleman with grey hair and a fancy little moustache as gray as his hair." [24] Under Colonel Bowie's stern guidance the infantry marched back and forth through the campgrounds and held target practice with Colt revolvers and Sharp carbines daily. The cavalry drilled on horseback along the bluff south of Ballona Creek. Colonel Bowie demanded sobriety and prohibited the sale of liquor within three miles of camp. Nevertheless, some of his soldiers continued to procure whiskey. After some investigation, the Colonel finally discovered the source: a fruit peddler, permitted to enter the

[21] *San Francisco Bulletin*, September 28, 1861.
[22] Hunt, *Army of the Pacific*, p. 40.
[23] *Southern News*, October 2, 1861; Hunt, *Army of the Pacific*, p. 41.
[24] Hunt, p. 41.

camp, had ingeniously cut out the rinds of some of his water-melons and filled them with liquor, which he sold to the troops at quite a profit. Needless to say, the peddler lost his permit.[25] Three stages made a daily run between the camp and Los Angeles, affording citizens the opportunity to watch the military in action.[26]

While the volunteers were rounding into fighting order at Camp Latham, the army regulars were preparing for their departure to the East. Camp Fitzgerald was abandoned, and the troops temporarily moved into Los Angeles, Companies B and K of the 1st Dragoons setting up camp on Spring Street, Company H of the 4th Infantry being quartered on Main, near the south end of town.[27]

Meantime, there were a number of command changes. By order of General Sumner, a new Military District of Southern California was formed, and Colonel George Wright, a Ver-monter with 39 years of army service, was placed in com-mand. Sumner's first instructions to Wright, dated Septem-ber 30th, spelled out the former's concern with disloyalty in southern California and the Confederate threat in Arizona: "The secession party in the state numbers about 32,000 and they are very restless and zealous, which gives them great influence. They are congregating in the southern part of the state, and it is there they expect to continue their operations against the government. . . . Put a stop to all demonstrations in favor of the rebel government, or against our own. You will establish a strong camp at Warner's Ranch and take measures to make Fort Yuma perfectly secure."[28]

Major Carleton, who had been in San Francisco since early August training volunteers to guard the Overland Mail route, was given new orders to report to southern California, where he was to await further instructions. Upon arriving in New

[25] *Ibid.*, p. 32.
[26] *Southern News,* October 2, 1861.
[27] *Star,* October 12, 1861.
[28] O.R., Ser. I, Vol. L, Pt. 1, p. 643.

San Pedro, he was authorized to proceed to Camp Latham for the purpose of training a regiment of California Volunteers for desert duty, a hazardous campaign into Arizona and Texas. Carleton undertook the task with his usual diligence. To his officers Carleton issued emphatic instructions. Eight hours a day, "Drill! Drill! Drill! Make ground rounds every night to see if sentinels and guards are on duty. . . . See personally each day to the cleanliness of camp, persons, arms, equipment, and the messing of the men. Have proper lines drawn between officers and rank and file." [29] So well were they trained that General Wright later declared that he had never seen a finer body of troops than those raised in California. [30]

In response to General Sumner's instructions, and to facilitate the movement of troops and supplies to Arizona to meet the Confederate challenge, a camp was established at Warner's Ranch in mid-October. Major Edwin A. Rigg, with four companies of infantry, left New San Pedro on October 10th and within twelve days had the new camp set up. The first site selected was about a mile from the old adobe ranch house; later it was moved to Oak Grove because of the severity of winter storms. The camp was named in honor of Colonel, later General, George Wright. [31]

The command shake-up was just beginning. A telegram from the War Department on October 20th ordered General Sumner to leave at once for the eastern theater of war. Colonel Wright, who had been in command of the District of Southern California for less than a month, was instructed to proceed to San Francisco and take command of the Department of the Pacific. He was promoted to Brigadier General. The Southern California vacancy was filled by James Henry Carleton, now promoted to Colonel. [32]

[29] *O.R.*, Ser. I, Vol. L, Pt. 1, p. 862.
[30] Hunt, *Carleton*, p. 202.
[31] *Ibid.*, p. 203.
[32] *Ibid.*, p. 197.

Near the end of October, the regular troops who had been garrisoning Los Angeles and San Bernardino since mid-summer began moving toward New San Pedro, their places taken by California Volunteers. By early November, nine companies of the 1st Dragoons and 4th Infantry were encamped just outside the seaport town, awaiting steamer passage to Panama and the East. On November 4th the ocean steamer *Golden Gate*, enroute to Panama from San Francisco, rounded Point Fermin and dropped anchor three miles offshore. To the cheers—and tears—of citizens lining the shore, the troops marched down to Banning's wharf, boarded the small harbor steamer *Comet*, and were ferried out to the *Golden Gate*. The little *Comet* took most of the day to complete the transfer. As shadows lengthened and the sky turned crimson toward the west, the *Golden Gate*, her decks crowded with cheering soldiers, hoisted anchor and steamed off into the fading sunset.[33] Most of her military complement never again laid eyes on southern California; many were soon to lay down their lives fighting for the Union.

Others sailed south destined for the Confederacy. In October, Joseph Lancaster Brent, Los Angeles attorney and former Democratic state assemblyman, journeyed north to San Francisco and boarded the *Orizaba*, bound for Panama. Joining him on board the ship were ex-senator William Gwin and Calhoun Benham, associate of Judge David S. Terry. All three men were bent on joining the Southern cause. By coincidence, General Sumner and his staff, along with a number of regular army officers, were aboard the same steamer. A few days before reaching Panama, Gwin and Brent made the mistake of approaching several of Sumner's officers in an effort to persuade them to join the Confederate ranks. Upon being informed of this, General Sumner angrily ordered Gwin, Brent, and Benham to the captain's cabin, where he notified them of their arrest on treason charges. But he made the mistake

[33] *Star*, November 9, 1861.

of allowing them to remain in their rooms instead of in confinement. Whereupon the threesome promptly returned to their cabins and dumped overboard all incriminating documents and letters, thereby depriving the government of evidence. Shortly after reaching New York, all three were released. Benham and Brent journeyed south and joined the Confederate Army, Brent eventually rising to the rank of Brigadier General. Gwin spent some time in Mississippi before going to France to labor fruitlessly for the recognition of the Confederacy.[34]

Many more tried to reach the Confederacy via the overland route. Already mentioned was the successful escape of the Ridley party and General Albert Sidney Johnston. But after the establishment of Camp Wright, the reenforcement of Fort Yuma, and increased vigilance on the part of the California Volunteers, this avenue of escape was considerably more difficult of passage.

Dan Showalter, northern California assemblyman who had gained brief notoriety when he killed C. W. Piercy, assemblyman from San Bernardino County, in a duel over political differences, tried this overland route in November, 1861. However, thanks to J. J. Warner and other Union informers, Colonel Carleton gained knowledge of Showalter's planned flight. Warner wrote to Carleton twice, the first time early in November, informing him that there was a party of 28 men in El Monte awaiting Showalter's arrival, the second time on November 11th, to the effect that Showalter and about 20 secessionists had just left Los Angeles enroute to Texas.[35] Before receiving the second Warner note, Carleton instructed the garrisons at Camp Wright and San Bernardino to be on the lookout for the assemblyman and State Supreme Court

[34] Bancroft, p. 284, footnote; Elijah R. Kennedy, *The Contest for California in 1861* (Boston: Houghton Mifflin Co., 1912), pp. 228–229. Kennedy's major assumption of a Confederate plot to take over California has been discredited by recent historians, but his book still contains much information of value.

[35] *O.R.*, Ser. I, Vol. L, Pt. 1, pp. 698, 717.

Judge David S. Terry, also thought to be escaping overland.[36] Carleton then sent a positive order to Fort Yuma: "Mr. Showalter with a party of Texans from El Monte will attempt to cross the desert; so, too, doubtless, Judge Terry. Give me a good account of these two men. . . . The time has gone by when matters are to be minced . . . with such open and avowed traitors." [37]

Probably unknown to Showalter, the net was closing on him. Cavalry patrols from San Bernardino and Camp Wright scoured the valleys and hills of the southern California back country. The search was for a time fruitless, until on November 28th, a patrol from Camp Wright, under Lieutenant Chauncey R. Wellman, learned in Temecula that a party of 16 men had spent the previous night there and departed that morning, heading southeast. Wellman and his men located and followed the unknown party's trail, heading for Warner's Ranch. After a night's dry bivouac, the soldiers again took up the chase. They had not gone far when they noticed smoke near a small ranch owned by a man named Winter and proceeded to investigate. At 8:30 in the morning of November 29th, Showalter and his 15 associates found themselves looking straight into the muzzles of Wellman's carbines. The two forces were almost evenly matched—Wellman's patrol numbered 18—and for a time the situation was touch and go. Wellman demanded the Showalter group accompany his to Camp Wright, while Showalter loudly protested that they were peaceful miners heading for Sonora to prospect. The argument was soon settled with the timely arrival of a strong detachment of infantry from Camp Wright. Hopelessly out-

---

[36] *Ibid.*, pp. 699–700. They were wrong about Judge Terry's being with Showalter. Terry was reported in El Monte in November, but then returned to San Francisco and later took ship to Panama and the Confederacy. See A. Russell Buchanan, *David S. Terry of California: Dueling Judge* (San Marino: The Huntington Library, 1956), pp. 129–131.

[37] *O.R., Ibid.*, pp. 699–700.

numbered, Showalter and his party now had no choice but to accompany the soldiers to camp.[38]

Showalter and his men were unable to persuade the Camp Wright temporary commander, Captain Hugh A. Gorley, that they were nothing more than peaceful miners. The camp garrison suddenly was placed on full alert when a report reached them that an oath-bound band of 75 men—probably Knights of the Golden Circle—was being assembled in El Monte for the express purpose of rescuing Showalter and his companions. Nothing came of this rumor, but the Union authorities remained in a jittery mood. On December 9th, General Wright issued and order that the Showalter group was to be held and securely guarded until further notice. At the army's request, the 16 pseudo-miners agreed to take an oath of allegiance to the United States; this was obviously done only with the intent of gaining their freedom, for they broke their word at the first opportunity. But the camp commander still would not release them without specific authority from General Wright. In December Showalter and his men were taken under heavy guard to Fort Yuma, where they were held for several months. Finally, in April 1862, the prisoners were directed to sign a second loyalty oath, which they did readily, and a few days later General Wright authorized the release of the entire group. Showalter then dropped from sight for a year; Union authorities were notified in February 1863 that he was a colonel in the Texas cavalry.[39]

All in all, Los Angeles County allegedly provided more than 250 fighting men for the Confederate Army, all but a few of them escaping California via the overland route.[40] In contrast, according to Major Horace Bell, only two local men

---

[38] Clarence C. Clendenen, "Dan Showalter—California Secessionist," *C.H.S. Quarterly*, December 1961. This is an excellent and absorbing account of Showalter's Civil War career.

[39] *Ibid.*

[40] Walters, p. 51.

actually fought in the East on the Union side, Bell himself
and Charles Jenkins.[41] And Jenkins was obliged to travel to
San Francisco before he dared enlist in the Union Army, so
strong was local anti-Union sentiment at the war's outbreak.[42]
However, 276 Los Angeles County citizens did respond to
Lincoln's call and join the California Volunteers for duty in
the West, so the balance sheet is nearly even.[43]

[41] Horace Bell, *On The Old West Coast* (New York: Grosset & Dunlap, 1930),
p. 74
[42] Walters, p. 48.
[43] Hunt, *Army of the Pacific*, p. 29.

STORM CLOUDS

THE NEW YEAR, 1862, was ushered in with leaden skies and drenching rain. A dark canopy of cumulo-nimbus clouds moved relentlessly in, wave after wave, and piled high against the abrupt rampart of the San Gabriel Mountains. Day after day, starting the last week of December, the land was pelted with sheets of rain, and snow piled deep on the mountains. Throughout most of January the storm continued. The Arroyo Seco, the Los Angeles and San Gabriel rivers swelled into angry torrents of muddy-brown water and overflowed their banks, inundating miles of lowland. Bridges were washed out, roads became impassable quagmires, cattle drowned, vineyards and farms were destroyed. In Los Angeles the business district was flooded. The merchants on Mellus Row labored frantically in waist-high water to save their inventories before the walls caved in. Adobe structures simply dissolved. And there seemed no end to nature's fierce deluge.[1]

A storm of another kind worried Colonel Carleton. Brigadier General Henry H. Sibley, Confederate commander in the Southwest, cast his eyes westward toward opening communications with southern California, where he believed the population "favorably inclined."[2] On January 27th, Sibley ordered Captain Sherod Hunter and a force of Texas cavalry to oc-

---

[1] *Star*, January 4, 11, 18, 25, 1862; Newmark, p. 309.
[2] *O.R.*, Ser. I, Vol. IV, pp. 169–170; see also Watford, p. 135.

cupy Tuscon. Hunter's force reached Tuscon on February 28th and was hailed by almost the entire population in an emotional outburst of Confederate sentiment. One observer noted, however, that any troops, Union or Confederate, who could give protection against the Apaches would have been well received there.[3] In the next few weeks, Captain Hunter's troops moved westward along the southern overland route to the Pima Villages, and small scouting detachments probed to within fifty miles of Fort Yuma and the Colorado.[4] Rumors circulated in Los Angeles that a Confederate force numbering 5,000 (in truth Hunter had about 100 men) was advancing on Fort Yuma and that California was "in imminent danger of invasion."[5]

In response to Confederate threats, real or imagined, Fort Yuma was reenforced with three companies of California Volunteers under Lieutenant Colonel Joseph R. West, lately of Camp Latham. Boats and ferries on the Colorado River were seized and guarded, and civilians forbidden to cross the river without army authorization.[6]

Colonel Carleton, meantime, was about to embark on an expedition that was destined to bring him fame (at least among Southwest historians). In December 1861, he had been instructed by General Wright to prepare and lead a strong force of California Volunteers to reopen the southern mail route, recapture Arizona for the Union, and link up with Brigadier General E. R. S. Canby in New Mexico.[7] For two months (as noted in the previous chapter) Carleton put his Volunteers through vigorous training at Camp Latham. In January his troops were ready to move, but the stormy weather which deluged southern California forced a postponement. No freight wagons could move out of Los Angeles or New San Pedro, nor could the 1,500 toughened soldiers of Carleton's California Column without first supplying the

---

[3] *O.R.*, Ser. I, Vol. IX, pp. 707, 868; Watford, p. 135.
[4] Watford, pp. 136–137.
[5] *Star*, February 22, 1862; *Southern News*, February 26, 1862.

forward bases. The Colonel, aware of Confederate successes in Arizona, displayed remarkable equanimity as he watched the hovering clouds gradually break up, the flood waters slowly recede, and the roads begin to dry out. "His sympathy was for his men who slept in rain-soaked blankets and leaky tents; and for the horses as they slushed through the muck in the corral or mired knee-deep in the pasture."[8]

Well before the land had dried enough for travel and the Los Angeles and San Gabriel rivers became fordable for wagons, Carleton was able to send messengers on sturdy horses to advanced units of his California Volunteers at Fort Yuma. The latter, along with some cavalry detachments that managed to get through from San Bernardino, were instructed to probe the Confederate positions in Arizona to discover their disposition and strength. While engaged in this effort, and in an attempt to rescue Captain William McCleave, who had been captured by Hunter and his Confederates at the Pima Villages, a vanguard force of the California Volunteers exchanged shots with a detachment of Texas troopers near Stanwix Station, an abandoned Butterfield Overland Stage post about 80 miles east of Fort Yuma. This mid-March action, miniscule in comparison with Bull Run or Gettysburg, was the westernmost skirmish of the Civil War.[9] One Californian was slightly injured in the engagement.

During February and early March, the California Volunteers at Camp Latham continued their vigorous training, now restless and eager for some kind of action. Steamer after steamer rounded Point Fermin and anchored in San Pedro Bay, depositing at Banning's wharf volunteers fresh out of

[6] Watford, p. 136.

[7] Hunt, *Carleton*, pp. 197–198.

[8] *Ibid.*, p. 211.

[9] Jay J. Wagoner, *Early Arizona: Prehistory to Civil War* (Tucson: University of Arizona Press, 1975), p. 454. Most Civil War historians are apparently unaware of the engagement at Stanwix Station and incorrectly detail the battle at Picacho Pass, 40 miles farther east, fought April 15, 1862, as the westernmost Civil War skirmish.

training camps in Sacramento, Oakland, and San Francisco. These new arrivals were initially quartered in tents on a low, sandy plain about a half mile out of New San Pedro. After the rains of January inundated the site, the troops were moved to higher ground about one mile northwest of town. On January 13, 1862, before the move was completed, the new army post was named Camp Drum, in honor of Major Richard C. Drum, adjutant-general of the Department of the Pacific.[10]

At last, in mid-March, Colonel Carleton was ready to send his California Volunteers, 1,500 strong, to Fort Yuma. Piecemeal, company by company, the proud Volunteers departed Camps Latham and Drum, marching one or two days apart to conserve water in the desert wells. Through Los Angeles, eastward to Chino Ranch, southeast through the chaparral-coated hills and valleys, verdant from the winter rains, to Temecula and Warner's Ranch, and finally the final leg through the inhospitable desert to Fort Yuma, moved the soldiers in blue, most on foot, the cavalry on their mounts, accompanied by Phineas Banning's huge freight wagons loaded down with equipment and supplies. It was a brutal march for those on foot; one infantryman wrote, "I have often heard the groans of the heavily loaded pack mules moving past on their way to the mountains, but never did I sympathize with them until I threw the burden off my back and rolled in the desert sand after a twenty-mile march."[11]

Colonel Carleton followed with the last contingent, departing Camp Drum on April 13th, just a few days before the birth of his second daughter, Maude. He was to forego the delight of seeing his child for several years. The Colonel was still in the desert, three days out of Fort Yuma, when he was promoted to Brigadier General of Volunteers, and honor he knew nothing about until late June, when he was halfway to

---

[10] Hunt, *Army of the Pacific*, pp. 42–43.
[11] *Sacramento Union*, May 23, 1862, cited in Hunt, *Carleton*, p. 215.

the Rio Grande. He reached Fort Yuma on the 1st of May, stayed two weeks to insure all was in readiness for his Southwest campaign, then with his 2,000-man California Column set out eastward to reconquer Arizona and, concurrently, to move out of the pages of southern California history.[12]

With General Carleton's California Column now threading its way across Arizona, life at Camps Latham and Drum settled down to normal garrison duty. There were several hundred California Volunteers at each camp, whose main duty was to keep Los Angeles and southern California secure for the Union.

Camp Drum actually had its origin in October 1861, soon after Carleton took command of the Military District of Southern California. Probably influenced by Phineas Banning and desirous of a location close to the harbor wherein his supplies and equipment arrived from San Francisco, Carleton then decided to make New San Pedro into the major army base and supply depot in southern California. After the before-mentioned abortive attempt to build the camp on low ground close to town, the army located a much better site on higher ground to the northwest. For the consideration of one dollar, Phineas Banning and Benjamin D. Wilson deeded to the United States three parcels of land, covering about 27 acres, where all the necessary buildings could be erected for the new camp and depot.[13]

Benjamin Wilson, former Los Angeles mayor and a major land-owner in southern California, was a political enigma to his friends. His Civil War loyalties were, at best, ambiguous. He and Banning supported the Union cause by donating the large tract near New San Pedro for Camp Drum, yet his sympathies, and those of his second wife, southern-born Margaret Hereford, were known to lie with the Confederacy. All his political life he had been a staunch Democrat, supporting the

---

[12] Hunt, *Carleton*, pp. 215–217.
[13] Hunt, *Army of the Pacific*, pp. 42–43.

pro-Southern Chivalry wing of the party during the pre-Civil War strife. He was the confidant of several rabid southern California secessionists such as Dr. John S. Griffin and Colonel Edward J. C. Kewen.[14] Perhaps he was truly divided in his loyalties, or, possibly, he was hedging his bets so that no matter which side won his interests would be secure.

Phineas Banning, on the other hand, left no question as to his loyalties—there was no stronger supporter of the Union cause in all of southern California. He was also an ambitious man who, partly for local pride, partly to further his own interests, desired to see New San Pedro become *the* number one seaport in the southern half of the state, as well as a major commercial center. With Camp Drum nearby, Banning obtained an enviable business advantage over his competitors. During the next few years, Banning's wagon trains hauled military supplies and equipment all over the Southwest; his steamers plied the waters of the Gulf of California and the lower Colorado with cargoes and soldiers for Fort Yuma and Arizona.[15]

New San Pedro, soon to be known as Wilmington, grew and prospered. A volunteer stationed at Camp Drum quite aptly described the town in April, 1862: "The town consists of Banning's residence, blacksmith shop, soap and tallow factory, coal and lumber yard, jerked beef jerkery, and a steam 'crawfish' that totes soldiers, baggage and mules five miles from the boats to his wharf when the tide is up. When the tide is out, he waits for the moon to work on the water. . . . The distance to anywhere from here is twenty miles, no roads, no fences, no houses intervening."[16]

In a few months of feverish construction work, Camp Drum developed from a primitive tent camp into a modern, handsome army post with permanent wood buildings. Lumber for

---

[14] John Walton Caughey, "Don Benito Wilson: An Average Southern Californian," *Huntington Library Quarterly*, Vol. II (1939), pp. 285–300.

[15] Krythe, *Port Admiral*, pp. 108–114; Hunt, *Army of the Pacific*, p. 43.

[16] *Southern News*, April 18, 1862.

the buildings was shipped around Cape Horn; and the construction costs were estimated to be a million dollars, quite a sum for that day. The officers' quarters was a two-story, sixteen room house, while five barracks, thirty by eighty feet, housed the enlisted men. Each building had a veranda in front and a large wing in the rear for kitchen and mess hall. The hospital was a large two-story, double-winged structure. In addition there were other buildings for the commissary, quartermaster, granary, store room, blacksmith shop, and guard house, and stables and corrals, all enclosed by a neat-looking picket fence. In addition, down by the steamboat landing in New San Pedro were the depot buildings and warehouses. The most substantial structure was the powder magazine, made of stone and cement with a heavy iron door.[17]

Soon after completion, the large army post became known as Drum Barracks, rather than Camp Drum. One Volunteer officer, upon arriving at the post from northern California, was surprised and pleased with what he saw: "We were astonished to find Drum Barracks one of the finest we had ever seen. Some of the men in our company who had seen service in the East said that they had never seen anything like it."[18]

Drum Barracks, as the military headquarters for southern California and Arizona, was an active and usually crowded post for the remainder of the Civil War. It was a rendezvous for recruits and troops bound for Fort Yuma and Arizona, and served as a depot for supplies, equipment, guns, and ammunition. One authority has estimated that the number of soldiers at Drum Barracks during most of the war years varied from 2,000 to 7,000.[19] The post was expected to send immediate

---

[17] Hunt, *Army of the Pacific*, pp. 43–44; Society for the Preservation of Drum Barracks, *Drum Barracks and The Camel Corps* (6 page pamphlet, 1965); and E. C. Colburn, "Swank Drum Barracks—It Saved the Union," *Westways*, March 1942.

[18] Hunt, *ibid.*, pp. 44–45.

[19] Society for the Preservation of Drum Barracks, p. 1.

relief to any part of the military district threatened by Confederates, secessionists, or Indians.

Early in 1862 the 31 camels of Lieutenant Beale's experimental Camel Corps—first stationed at Fort Tejon, then in Los Angeles—moved to Drum Barracks, occasioning great excitement and curiosity among the local populace. Efforts to utilize the beasts as a "Dromedary Line" between Drum Barracks, Los Angeles, Fort Mojave, an other points proved a failure, and in September 1863 Secretary of War Stanton ordered all the army camels sold at public auction. Those at Drum Barracks were herded to Benicia, where they were sold to private individuals.[20]

The soldiers stationed at Drum Barracks occasionally got 48-hour furloughs to visit Los Angeles. Those fortunate enough to get time off usually walked into New San Pedro, boarded one of Banning's new stages, and rode north on San Pedro Road, more of a rutted cowpath than a highway. About two hours of jarring travel across a vast prairie, usually dotted with grazing horses and cattle, were required to reach their destination. Los Angeles, one of them wrote, "looks like the ruins of a fine city. The three and four-story brick buildings in the heart of the city and the one-story adobes in the outskirts present a queer contrast. Some of the adobes are so old that only one room remains of what was once large buildings."[21]

Camp Latham, out west above Ballona Creek, was not as bustling as Drum Barracks, but its garrison of several hundred California Volunteers kept active by constant drill, patrol duty, and answering calls for help. In early 1862, an urgent plea came from white settlers in Owens Valley, 200 miles to the north. Resentful of intrusion by white miners and farmers, the Owens Valley Paiute rose in revolt, killed several settlers, and besieged others. In response, Lieutenant

[20] *Ibid.*
[21] Hunt, *Army of the Pacific*, p. 45.

Colonel George S. Evans and a detachment of the 2nd Cavalry, California Volunteers, left Camp Latham for the troubled desert valley on March 19, 1862. After rescuing a small group of settlers beseiged at Putnam's Fort, a strongly-built stone house and trading post near what later became the town of Independence, Evans continued north to the vicinity of Bishop Creek, Finding the Paiutes well entrenched in strong natural positions above the creek, Evans realized that an attempt to dislodge them would be suicidal. As the expedition was not equipped for an extensive campaign, he was obliged to retire from the valley, returning to Camp Latham on April 28th.

The Lieutenant Colonel reported the situation in Owens Valley as acute and recommended a permanent military post be established there. Early in June, General Wright ordered Evans back to Owens Valley, to establish an army camp in the vicinity of Pine Creek. On June 12th Evans again departed Camp Latham, this time with a strong force: 200 men of the 2nd Cavalry and a train of 46 wagons carrying supplies for a two-month campaign. Their destination, as ordered, was Pine Creek, near the present town of Big Pine, where Evans planned to locate a base camp for his campaign to subdue the Paiutes. The party reached Putnam's Fort at daylight, June 26th. They found nothing but ruins; the Indians had burned everything but the stone walls and carried away everything of value.

Evans rested a few days, then resumed his northward march. But the journey was now more difficult. From far above the valley, torrents churned downward from the rapidly melting snowpack of the Sierra Nevada crest. The resultant swelling of the Owens River and its many tributaries made it very difficult to get men and equipment across the larger water courses.

On July 4, 1862, Evans and his men reached Oak Creek, about four miles north of the present town of Independence.

Finding the creek a raging torrent, Evans decided to make his camp on a clearing above the south bank of the stream, twenty miles short of his original Pine Creek destination. The Colonel raised the Stars and Stripes over newly christened Camp Independence, named for the day on which it was founded. Henceforth, Drum Barracks would have one more army post to supply.[22]

[22] Helen S. Giffen, "Camp Independence—An Owens Valley Outpost," *H.S. S.C. Quarterly*, December 1942; Hunt, *Army of the Pacific*, pp. 254–256. See also this writer's "Camp Independence," *Desert Magazine*, October 1969.

Camel at Drum Barracks, 1863

*Same view with camel retouched, U.S. Army Headquarters
at Wilmington, loading camel at warehouse*

"MORE VIGOROUS MEASURES"

Los Angeles buzzed with excitement as winter's wet chill gave way to spring's clear skies and verdant landscape. News of the Confederates in Arizona and the progress of the California Column filled the pages of the local press, but the really big stories concerned a golden bonanza at La Paz on the Colorado River. "Ho! For the Colorado!" became a common exuberation as would-be prospectors outfitted themselves and left town by the score, following William Bradshaw's new road across the desert to the mines. A sizeable portion of the Mexican population drifted away for the river and its promised riches. In May, the *Star* announced that at least $12,000 in gold, including a nugget as large as a hen's egg, had reached Los Angeles from the Colorado diggings.[1]

In Los Angeles, the Unionists, who so far had little to cheer about, were electrified when the steamer *Wright* brought them good tidings of General U. S. Grant's capture of Fort Donelson in Tennessee. A bonfire was kindled on Main Street and the old cannon was brought forth at the Plaza to fire a few victory salutes. "After firing several rounds, the cannon, being old and rusty, exploded, fortunately hurting no one.

[1] *Star*, May 17, 1862; see also Harold and Lucile Weight, "Forgotten Road to Gold," *Westerners Brand Book*, Book Ten (Los Angeles: Los Angeles Corral, Westerners, 1963), pp. 11–33.

But this accident did not deter our Union men, who procured anvils and kept up the firing till long after midnight."[2]

While the *Southern News* was heralding the Union triumphs, few as they were in 1862, Hamilton continued his tirade against Lincoln's war: " . . . we can look upon it as no other than an abolition war, instigated, carried on, and to be consummated, by the degredation of the white race, and the elevation of the African family over them."[3]

Statements such as this, along with many other diatribes against the government, were bound to get the *Star* in trouble with the Union authorities—particularly in time of war. Late in February, a dispatch from the Postmaster's Office in Washington reached Los Angeles to the effect that "Orders have been issued for the suppression of the *Oregon Democrat, Los Angeles Star,* and *California Star* from the mail, on the ground that they have been used for the purpose of overthrowing the Government, giving aid and comfort to the enemy now at war with the United States Government."[4] Later Los Angeles postmaster W. G. Still received the following order from the First Assistant Postmaster General in Washington:

Post Office Department
February 14, 1862

It is appearing to this Department that the Los Angeles Star, a newspaper published at Los Angeles, Cal., is used for the purpose of overthrowing the Government of the United States; it is therefore ordered that said paper be excluded from all post offices and mails of the United States, until further notice.

By order of the P. M. General

(signed) KASSON
First Ass't. P. M. General[5]

[2] *Southern News,* February 28, 1862.
[3] *Star,* January 11, 1862.
[4] *Star,* March 1, 1862; *Southern News,* February 28, 1862.
[5] *Southern News,* April 9, 1862.

Wilmington Exchange Building and Hotel Stage for Los Angeles, 1863

Hamilton was furious. He flatly denied the allegation that he was trying to overthrow the Government, argued that the Lincoln administration's claims of upholding liberties of speech and press "are mere shams ... a weak effort by a strong government." He further boasted that being banned from the mails would have little effect on the newspaper's circulation, since it would be carried by private conveyance in the southern counties and it had few subscribers elsewhere.[6] Hamilton was apparently correct in this last claim, as there was no noticeable disruption in the *Star's* local distribution, nor any change in its editorial policies.[7]

That Hamilton was not in the least intimidated by the government's action was evident in the next issue of the *Star*. A letter from someone who called himself "Jayhawk" was printed, sarcastically critical of the Lincoln administration's action: "His Majesty Abraham I has seen proper to proscribe your paper.... Why speak of the Constitution now at all? The tool of abolitionism who now disgraces the chair of Washington, under the pretense of trying to force others to the observance of the Constitution of the United States, has virtually set it aside himself ... by his dictatorial decree putting down the liberty of the press."[8]

Slightly more than a month after the government banned what it considered disloyal newspapers from the mails, a policy of harassment of secessionist sympathizers was initiated in southern California. The apparent instigator of this local crackdown was Henry D. Barrows, United States Marshal for the Southern District. On April 9, 1862, Barrows wrote an urgent letter to Colonel Carleton, commander of the Southern California Military District, requesting military aid "to assist me in arresting and detaining the person of A. J. King, the present Under Sheriff of this county." Barrows' complaint, and the basis for the arrest order, was that Deputy

[6] *Star*, March 1, 1862.
[7] Rice, p. 233.
[8] *Star*, March 8, 1862.

Sheriff King had "brought into this city [Los Angeles] and ostentatiously displayed before a large crowd of citizens an elegantly engraved and framed lithographic portrait, life size, of the rebel General Beauregard," and further, "in my presence has disavowed all allegiance to our National Government, at the same time proclaiming that Jeff Davis is the only constitutional government that we have."[9]

In response to Barrows' request, a detachment of cavalry arrested King at his Los Angeles Sheriff's Office and escorted him to Drum Barracks. His confinement, however, was brief; he was released after taking an oath of allegiance to the United States.[10]

Henry Barrows was quite unhappy about Deputy Sheriff King's quick release. He addressed a strong protest to General Wright in San Francisco, complaining that the Army's policy in regard to secessionists in California was not aggressive enough, and asked, "May not the Union citizens of this section ask that greater rigor be exercised toward secessionism, or the expression of it, in Southern California? It permeates society here among both high and low. Our local State, county, and city officers, with very few exceptions, are avowed sympathizers with it. It is popular here, and the Union Cause is very generally despised. Union men feel that they cannot live here if something is not done to attack and destroy secessionism here, which is strong, insidious, and specious, and far too crafty for the policy that would do nothing against it unless it be a clear case of some overt act, that policy is utterly inadequate. . . . I beseech you in behalf of the handful of sincere Union men in this community to have the strings drawn tauter here on that insidious secessionism against which Union policy too often is no match."[11]

Barrows' plea evidently shocked General Wright into adopting—at least temporarily—stronger measures against seces-

[9] *O.R.*, Ser. I, Vol. L, Pt. 1, pp. 993–994.
[10] *Ibid.*, p. 994; *Southern News*, April 11, 1862.
[11] *Ibid.*, pp. 996–998.

sionists in southern California. On April 19th, he wrote the
United States Attorney that, "I shall not hesitate a single
moment in using the most stringent measures for the suppression of treason or disloyalty to our Government, and the officers in command of U. S. Troops will arrest and hold in
confinement all persons against whom such charges can well
be established." [12]

Four days later, Wright issued his General Order No. 17,
stating that the army would adopt "more vigorous measures"
to suppress treason in the state. "Treason's hideous crest shall
not pollute the fair land of California. Military commanders
will promptly arrest and hold in custody all persons against
whom the charge of aiding and abetting the rebellion can be
sustained; and under no circumstances will such persons be
released without first subscribing the oath of allegiance to the
United States." [13]

Even before General Wright's "more vigorous measures"
order was announced, rumors circulated in Los Angeles that
the Union authorities were making a list of proscribed persons to be taken into custody as suspected traitors; among
those alleged to be on the "black list" were John Rains, proprietor of Rancho Cucamonga, Dr. James Winston of the Bella
Union Hotel, and Dr. John S. Griffin, brother-in-law of Confederate General Albert Sidney Johnston. Judge Benjamin
Hayes, a highly respected member of the community, was
apprehensive about this secret list and expressed the fear
that "we are on the eve of witnessing serious evils in this
beautiful section of the state." Hayes believed Jonathan Warner and the local Union Club were behind the intimidation
effort, and declared that "the chief object is to fan the flame
of civil disorder in our community." [14]

Although a number of suspected rebel sympathizers were
taken into custody during the next two and a half years, no

12 *Ibid.*, p. 1015.
13 *Ibid.*, pp. 1021–1022.
14 Hayes, pp. 262–263.

reign of terror developed. Most suspects were released immediately upon taking the oath of allegiance, and only a few were confined as long as a month. Probably most responsible for this moderation policy was General Wright, Commander of the Department of the Pacific. Wright ordered strict measures to suppress any disturbances, but did not believe in being unduly harsh. His lenient attitude earned him the vituperation of ultra loyalists, who accused him of catering to the secessionists and went so far as to petition the War Department for his removal.[15] Wright, in defending his actions, claimed that his policy was "fully endorsed by the sensible portion of the community. . . . Were I to be guided by the dictates of the radical press I should crowd my forts with men charged with disloyalty, keep this country in constant ferment. . . . These radicals seem to believe that it is my special duty to arrest every man or woman whose sentiments do not coincide exactly with the Government."[16]

Harris Newmark recalled, years later, that "Men on both sides grew hotheaded and abused one another roundly, but few bones were broken and little blood was shed. A policy of leniency was adopted by the authorities, and sooner or later persons arrested for political offenses were discharged."[17]

The war raged on in the East, its full fury revealed to local citizens on the front pages of the *Star* and *Southern News.* In May, many citizens were grieved to learn of the death of General Albert Sidney Johnston in the terrible Battle of Shiloh. The late Confederate general was well known in Los Angeles; his widow and five children lived here with Dr. Griffin. The *Star* printed the full text of Jefferson Davis' memorial speech on Johnston, along with many local tributes to the fallen soldier.[18]

[15] Joseph Ellison, *California and the Nation, 1850–1869: A Study of the Relations of a Frontier Community with the Federal Government* (Berkeley: University of California Press, 1927), p. 203.
[16] *O.R.*, Ser. I, Vol. L, Pt. 2, pp. 846–847.
[17] Newmark, p. 299.
[18] *Star*, May 24 and 31, 1862.

Unionists in town were pleased to learn that the Bella Union was under new management, leased by John King and Henry Hummil. The *News* rejoiced that "a large American flag has been hoisted over the house, and we hope that the stigma which has been attached to the house will be removed, as the present proprietors . . . are sound Unionists."[19] No longer would the city's largest hotel be a secessionist hangout.

The Fourth of July, 1862, passed with little notice in Los Angeles. Several irrepressible Union lovers did rise with the sun, raise the flag over the Court House, and fire a salute of 34 guns from the hill behind the Plaza. The latter action provoked a negative response from local secessionists, and rebel yells were heard throughout town. "We blush for Los Angeles," said the *News*, "when we state . . . that the proceedings awoke the 'disgust' and called forth remarks from some."[20]

Most of the staunch Unionists in town spent the day out at Camp Latham, where a day-long celebration of the glorious Fourth was observed. In the morning there was a grand review of the troops, in full dress, accompanied by martial music. After a noontime salute of 34 guns, various officers took turns reading the Declaration of Independence, Washington's Farewell Address, and other patriotic orations, which produced "many outbursts of enthusiasm." The band then rang out with "Hail Columbia" and "The Star Spangled Banner." There followed a collation and a dinner hour "interwoven with patriotic sentiment, sweet music, etc., etc." At 3 p.m. citizens and soldiers promenaded through the willow grove across Ballona Creek, and at 5 the festivities were concluded with another 34-gun salute. "The road was lined with coaches, carriages, etc., homeward bound, wrapped in thought, and impressed with patriotic emotions long to be remembered."[21]

[19] *Southern News*, June 4, 1862.
[20] *Ibid.*, July 9, 1862.
[21] *Ibid.*

A NEWSPAPER'S TIRADE

READERS OF THE *Los Angeles Star* might be excused if they gained the impression that President Lincoln was a tyrant and a bumpkin. In editorial after editorial, week after week, Henry Hamilton climbed all over the President's back, damned his administration and Republicans in general, and severely criticized his underlings. The editor of the *Star* gave no quarter, and obviously asked none. His war against Lincoln was a holy war, waged in defense of Hamilton's ideas of the Constitution, the sacred rights of Americans, and white supremacy.

In the summer of 1862, Hamilton focused his outrage on Lincoln's war tax. "Hundreds of millions of dollars have to be raised, to support waste and extravagance of maintaining half a million men as food for powder," he thundered.[1] Hamilton was certain that a clique of New York abolitionists was pulling the federal strings, and Lincoln, through ignorance or design, was singing their tune. He was certain that Lincoln's purpose in waging bloody war on the South was the abolition of slavery, and arming Negroes to rape and murder their white masters. Black Republican rule, he thought, "has degenerated into worse than an oriental despotism."[2]

The *News*, now an avid supporter of Lincoln and the Union, called Hamilton's continuous tirade pure and simple

---

[1] *Star*, July 26, 1862.
[2] *Ibid.*, August 23, 1862.

treason. "For more than a year, a paper published in this city, conducted by an Irishman, has teemed with articles abusive of the Government and its officers, and misrepresenting the object and aim for which the war is waged." The paper saw a distinct difference between free speech and sedition. "No other Government in the world suffers itself to be misrepresented and maligned by its citizens, and it is time our Government should prove no exception."[3]

Politics once again took the spotlight as the long days of August drew to a close, and Hamilton was right in the thick of the battle. The *Star* gave full coverage, and voiced agreement, to the resolutions passed at the Democratic State Convention in Sacramento. To the delight of Hamilton, the Democrats were strongly anti-war: "We are opposed to the employment of force by the General Government against the seceded States, for the purpose of compelling obedience and submission to Federal authority." The convention further went on record as favoring a reunited Union if acceptable to both warring parties, but if not, the recognition of the Confederate States as a sovereign nation. The slogan adopted by the Democrats and seconded by the *Star* was "The Constitution as it is, the Union as it was."[4]

Los Angeles County Democrats assembled a week later at the Court House, supported the candidates and platform of the State Convention, and selected candidates for county and local offices. Two outspoken secessionists were chosen for state assembly: Colonel E. J. C. Kewen and J. A. Watson. The *Star* gave its support to the ticket and urged its readers to "Man the guns—give the Black cohorts of Abolition a broadside, and disperse them to the winds."[5]

The election on September 3rd resulted in the usual Democratic victory in Los Angeles County, although the margin

[3] *Southern News*, July 30, 1862.
[4] *Star*, August 16, 23, 30, 1862.
[5] *Ibid.*, August 30, 1862.

was closer than usual. The *Star* blamed this on emigration to the Colorado River mines and an "outrage of the Military" at the Ballona precinct. According to the *Star*, soldiers from Camp Latham seized the ballot boxes of the precinct, dispensed with the duly appointed civilian officials, and stuffed the ballot boxes with the illegal votes of over 200 non-resident California Volunteers. Further, citizens of known Democratic inclination were allegedly driven off by "300 bayonets" and refused their right to vote.[6]

Likewise, according to the *Star*, the New San Pedro precinct "earned for itself an unenviable notoriety for rowdyism during the election" by intimidating voters of Democratic sentiment and not permitting many of them to cast a ballot. "One gentleman, determined to assert his rights of an American citizen, presented his ballot with one hand, holding his pistol in the other. . . . We understand the cowardly mob attacked a gentleman of well known Democratic principles the night before election and drove him from the precinct."[7]

The returns from the Ballona and New San Pedro precincts seemed to bear out the *Star's* charges. Ballona gave 204 and 208 votes to the Union Party assembly candidates, Hayes and Johnson respectively, and only 6 and 2 votes for Kewen and Watson, Democrats. New San Pedro voted 92 and 91 for the two Union candidates, and 4 each for the Democratic candidates. Countywide, the Democratic assembly nominees were victorious by counts of 761 and 718 to 680 and 676 respectively, which prompted the *Star* to say, "Democracy have cause for self-gratulation, in the fact, notwithstanding all the bullying and illegal voting, their votes outnumbered the combinations formed against them."[8]

The Ballona vote, obviously a flagrant violation of the election laws, was voided by the County Board of Canvassers

[6] *Ibid.*, September 6 and 13, 1862.
[7] *Ibid.*, September 6, 1862.
[8] *Ibid.*

after a protest by Colonel Kewen and H. N. Alexander, the latter president of the Los Angeles County Democrats. The Board cited the army's seizure of the ballot boxes and the illegality of over 200 votes by non-resident soldiers as reasons for its action.[9]

A correspondent from the *San Francisco Bulletin*, in Los Angeles during the election, wrote, "Secesh has carried this county again, body and boots, for Dixie—despite the volunteers' votes, and despite the fact that a large number of the usually bought votes of the Democracy is now at the Colorado mines. . . . Unionism here is nowhere. To all intents and purposes, we might as well live in the Southern Confederacy as in Southern California."[10]

The days of Camp Latham, where the election irregularities occurred, drew to a close in October. The army camp above Ballona Creek was abandoned and its complement of California Volunteers removed to Drum Barracks near New San Pedro. Henceforth, the Union Army would have but one military base in Los Angeles County.[11]

Down at New San Pedro, Phineas Banning was unhappy about southern California's lack of support of the Sanitary Fund. This was an effort by the United States Sanitary Commission—forerunner of the American Red Cross—to raise money to aid wounded Union soldiers and their families. Northern Californians contributed generously to the Sanitary Fund, but efforts to raise money in the southern part of the state had so far amounted to nothing. Under Banning's initiative, New San Pedro raised $400 and Old San Pedro $100. Banning then journeyed to Los Angeles in an attempt to subscribe funds here. The *News* reported, "A subscription paper is being circulated in Los Angeles for alleviation of the sufferings of our sick and wounded soldiers. One hundred

[9] *Ibid.*, September 20, 1862.
[10] *San Francisco Bulletin*, September 15, 1862.
[11] *Southern News*, October 3, 1862.

dollars has already been paid in, and between three or four hundred dollars subscribed."[12]

Unable to win at the ballot box, Union authorities resorted to harsher tactics in an effort to suppress secessionism in Los Angeles. Early in October, Colonel Edward J. C. Kewen, newly elected to the state assembly, was arrested by a detachment of soldiers from Drum Barracks. The charge, as usual, was treason. Kewen, a Missourian with a fiery temper, and one of the few Los Angeles attorneys who did not go South to fight during the Civil War, was accused in an affidavit signed by three witnesses of cheering for Jeff Davis and other disloyal utterances. He was escorted to Drum Barracks, then shipped to the army's detention camp on Alcatraz Island. Kewen was confined there for two weeks, then allowed to take an oath of allegiance. After posting a $5,000 bond, he was released and allowed to return to Los Angeles. Upon arriving on the steamer *Senator*, he was warmly greeted by a number of friends, "showing plainly what a hold he has upon the affections of his fellow citizens," according to the *Star*.[13]

Dr. R. T. Hayes, Kewen's opponent in the recent election, filed a suit in District Court contesting Kewen's assembly seat on the grounds that the latter was not a U. S. citizen (Kewen was with William Walker on his Nicaraguan filibustering expedition and had lived in Central America for a number of years) and that Kewen was disloyal, "that you have on various occasions, and at different places, expressed yourself friendly to, and in favor of the existing rebellion."[14] Hayes' suit was quickly dismissed by the court.[15]

Just a week after Kewen's arrest, the Deputy U. S. Marshal in Los Angeles arrested Henry Hamilton, also on a charge of treason, and hustled him to Drum Barracks. Hamilton was

[12] *Southern News*, October 3, 1862; and Krythe, *Port Admiral*, pp. 118–119.

[13] *Star*, October 11, 18, 25, November 1, 8, 1862; and W. W. Robinson, *Lawyers of Los Angeles* (Los Angeles: Los Angeles Bar Association, 1959), p. 47.

[14] *Star*, October 11, 1862.

[15] *Ibid.*, November 1, 1862.

allowed no time to arrange for the continued publication of the *Star*, but his foreman was able to keep the paper going during the editor's enforced absence. From Drum Barracks, Hamilton was placed on a steamer bound for Alcatraz. The *News* hoped he would remain there until war's end, and declared that the *Star* was "one of the most and perhaps the most treasonable sheet in the loyal States." [16]

Hamilton was released ten days after his arrest. The *Star* informed its readers that he had not been incarcerated on Alcatraz, but had been placed in the charge of the army's provost marshal. Two weeks later Hamilton returned to Los Angeles, where he was promptly feted as the guest of honor at a barbecue given by the "warm hearted denizens of the Monte." [17]

If the Union authorities thought they had intimidated Henry Hamilton, they soon discovered that they were sadly mistaken. The *Star's* impenitent editor promptly stepped up his violent diatribes against the Lincoln administration.

Hamilton reserved his most bitter denunciation for Lincoln's Emancipation Proclamation, which the enraged editor labeled "the sorriest document which has ever emanated from an occupant of the eminent position." He then attacked the President with the assertion, "It is a disgrace to the American people that they should have elected to the Presidential chair a man so ill qualified for the lofty position as Mr. Lincoln." [18]

The *Star* often carried on its front page dissertations from other newspapers, both domestic and foreign, favorable to the Confederacy and attacking the Union administration. One displayed prominently, from the *Chicago Tribune*, was entitled "Is the Constitution Suspended During the War?" This was a strong denunciation of Lincoln's suspension of Habeas

---

[16] *News*, October 22 and 27, 1862. (After October 8, 1862, the *News* dropped "*Southern*" from its title.)

[17] *Star*, November 15, 1862.

[18] *Ibid.*, December 13, 1862.

Corpus, his use of martial law, and the Emancipation Proclamation.[19]

Hamilton appeared to be proud of Los Angeles citizens
fighting for the Confederacy, and frequently told of their
exploits. Some that were prominently mentioned were Alonzo
Ridley, General A. S. Johnston's bodyguard when the latter
fell at Shiloh, later with General Forest's cavalry; George W.
Gift, lieutenant in the Confederate Navy who saw action on
the Mississippi River; and Joseph Lancaster Brent, chief of
ordnance for General Magruder.[20]

In December 1862, Hamilton gave much attention to the
Battle of Fredericksburg, where the Union Army suffered a
serious defeat: "We give up our entire space to the details of
the great battle at Fredericksburg—we say battle, but it was
rather a massacre. . . . The Abolition force put forth its might-
iest energies, and it was defeated, totally routed, 'horse, foot, and
dragoons.' . . . Who can conceive the bereavements, the mourning, the wailing, the heart-breakings, in thousands of families, at the loss of their most valued members—and all this,
for no purpose; absolutely, for no purpose under God's heav-
en. . . . The rule of this abolition faction will not be forever.
It is doomed. The handwriting is discernable on the wall." [21]
As the year 1862 came to an end, Hamilton saw victory for
the Confederacy just around the corner, and likewise, the
triumph of everything he stood for: the Constitution, States
Rights, the "old" Democratic Party, and the supremacy of
the white man.

[19] *Ibid.*, December 27, 1862.
[20] *Ibid.*, November 29, 1862.
[21] *Ibid.*, December 27, 1862.

EPIDEMIC

THE DREADFUL SPECTER of disease cast a pall over Los Angeles during the winter of 1862–1863. Smallpox made its appearance in the final weeks of December and spread rapidly with the new year, principally among the Mexican and Indian population. By mid-January, when the scourge hit its peak in Los Angeles, as many as fourteen died in one day. The city's smallpox wagon—dubbed the "Black Maria"—was a frequent and disheartening sight as it rolled through the streets carrying victims to the city hospital, or "pesthouse," in Chavez Ravine. Deaths became so numerous that undertakers could hardly be secured to bury the victims, much less provide funeral services. The city council met in emergency session and appointed a board of health manned by local doctors. Dr. Russel T. Hayes, city surgeon, was ordered to vaccinate all persons; those that refused faced arrest. Los Angeles was divided into five districts, each district headed by a commissioner whose job was to inspect every house in his area. Infected premises were affixed with a yellow flag and quarantined. During the height of the epidemic, nearly every house in Sonora-town flew the dreaded flag. By early February there were 278 cases in town, and more than a hundred lay in their graves.

In February the disease spread to other parts of southern California. El Monte was hit badly. Many of the sick were hauled in wagons to San Gabriel Mission, the fortunate ones to receive medical attention and to pray, the unlucky victims to be buried in the mission graveyard. This lasted until El Monte officials objected to the gravely ill being carried through the streets of town and put a stop to the practice. San Juan Capistrano was severely affected. In San Bernardino County, whole Indian rancherías were depopulated, as the Indian method of treating disease—sweating, followed by a plunge in cold water—almost invariably produced fatal results. One of those stricken was Juan Antonio, the great Cahuilla chieftain.

The epidemic finally subsided in March, but not before exacting a fearsome toll. Dead were over half of the Indians of Los Angeles, and many in the outlying areas. What the white man's harshness had begun, the white man's disease completed.[1]

Smallpox or not, politics and the war went on as usual. The *Star* greeted the new year with a blast at the Emancipation Proclamation, which took effect on January 1st: "Of course, the feature of the season is, the day on which President Lincoln's abolition proclamation takes effect. By the stroke of his pen, Mr. Lincoln frees every slave in rebeldom, robs every master of his servant, every household of its property. Was ever such an outrage perpetuated in the name of law, or such foul perjury committed, as by this man, sworn to maintain the Constitution and govern by these laws."[2]

Hamilton was outraged by an incident in Visalia which he felt posed a threat to all California newspapers expressing anti-government views. For some months the *Visalia Equal Rights Expositor* had bitterly denounced the Lincoln adminis-

[1] *Star*, January 24, February 7 and 14, March 7, 1863; Newmark, p. 322; J. Albert Wilson, *History of Los Angeles County, California*; reproduction, (Berkeley: Howell–North, 1959), p. 97; Marco R. Newmark, "Medical Profession in the Early Days of Los Angeles," *H.S.S.C. Quarterly*, March 1952; Beattie, p. 403.

[2] *Star*, January 3, 1863.

tration and had been particularly caustic in its remarks about the President. Among the epithets thrown at Lincoln were "a narrow-minded bigot," "an unprincipled demagogue," "a drivelling, idiotic, imbecile creature," who "will die universally execrated." In October 1862, the army established Camp Babbit near Visalia to control secessionist activities in the area. Immediately the *Expositor* insulted the soldiers stationed there as "Lincoln's hirelings" who wore "Abe Lincoln's livery." On March 5, 1863, the *Expositor* published its last issue. An article abusive to army volunteers, entitled "California Cossacks," so infuriated the soldiers at Camp Babbitt and Union men in town that they decided to take matters in their own hands. That evening, a mob of 70 or 80 volunteers and loyal townsmen took just fifteen minutes to completely demolish the office of the secessionist newspaper, smash the press, and toss type, paper, and ink into the street.[3]

The *Star*, obviously concerned about its own safety, criticized the Unionist mob as "blinded by fanaticism and bigotry," and asked, "Do these dirty minions of a tyrannical power imagine that by the simple demolition . . . they are combatting error?"[4] Although there were fears expressed that a similar mob action might happen in Los Angeles, and a secessionist paper in Merced was destroyed the following year, no southern California newspaper was threatened or assaulted during the war.

Colonel Edward J. C. Kewen, Los Angeles' pro-Confederate assemblyman, earned a reputation in Sacramento that made his secessionist supporters in southern California proud. In April, the Colonel introduced a resolution opposing "unconstitutional measures and arbitrary acts" of the Lincoln administration, and another asserting that the war had failed and "the time for honorable pacification has arrived." As expected, with Union majorities controlling both houses of

[3] Gilbert, pp. 160–164.
[4] *Star*, March 28, 1863.

the state legislature, Kewen was shouted down when he tried to introduce his resolutions, and threatened with expulsion from the assembly. Although he remained in the legislature, he was decidedly unpopular among many of his lawmaking colleagues.[5]

Tragedy struck in San Pedro Bay on April 27, 1863. Late in the afternoon, Phineas Banning's little ferry steamer, the *Ada Hancock*, left Wilmington and made her way down the estuary, carrying her second load of San Francisco-bound passengers to the *Senator*, anchored five miles out. Along with the passengers, there were quite a number aboard taking the trip out to the ocean steamer for pleasure or to say goodbye to friends. In all, there were 53 persons on the *Ada Hancock*, plus her crew.

When the little vessel was about a mile from the wharf a sudden squall came up. The boat careened under the impact of the gale; sea water engulfed the boiler tubes, causing the boiler to explode. Twenty-six were killed outright, many were badly injured, and only seven aboard the ferry escaped unscathed. Prompt rescue efforts by local fishermen and Drum Barracks personnel kept the toll from climbing higher.

The confusion and terror were so great that three hours passed before word of the disaster reached Los Angeles. Upon hearing the news, the city's three doctors and scores of citizens rushed to Wilmington in "every vehicle and means of conveyance that could be obtained." They were greeted by a gruesome sight. The bodies of the dead were lined up on the wharf and in the warehouse, and the twenty injured were being cared for by local citizens and army personnel from Drum Barracks. Several of the dead were well-known southern Californians: Captain Seeley; wagon-master William Sanford; Tom Workman; and Miss Hereford, Benjamin Wilson's sister-in-law. A coroner's inquest found no culpability for the accident attached to the officers or to Banning, the

[5] *Star*, April 11 and 18, 1863.

boat's owner.Even though Banning was exonerated, he insisted upon paying the expenses of those injured, and recompensing the families of those who had been killed.[6]

Disloyaly was ever the concern of Union men in California, and as the war continued, new efforts were made to control the state's secessionist minority. Hindsight has indicated that these fears of Confederate subversion were gross exaggerations, but they seemed real to many California Unionists at the time, and the latter acted accordingly.

"National life," argued a Republican Party campaign appeal in 1862, "should be maintained and perpetuated ... by the ramification of test oaths into all departments of society —mechanical, mercantile, agricultural, and professional." Loyalty oaths received widespread application in the North during the Civil War, and California was quick to follow the national trend. Several leading California Republicans professed to believe that more should be done to insure the state's commitment to the Union. They were critical of General Wright for his alleged "excessively restrained suppression of Southern sympathizers," and felt the legislature should take strong action to "ferret out traitors in our midst." During the 1862 legislative session, Republicans attempted without success to pass loyalty oath laws, but this temporary failure served to fortify their determination. Strengthened as a result of the September 1862 state election, they tried once again. Early in 1863, Assemblyman J. J. Owen, Republican of Santa Clara, introduced "An Act to Exclude Traitors and Alien Enemies from the Courts of Justice in Civil Cases." By this measure—a frank imitation of an oath required by Congress for federal civil and military officers—lawyers and litigants were required to file affidavits of allegiance to the federal government before they were allowed to engage in civil cases. Democrats called it "A Black Republican test oath," and were generally opposed to it, but the Unionist-dominated legislature

[6] *Star*, May 2, 1863; Krythe, *Port Admiral*, pp. 115–117.

passed the act in April, 1863.[7] Los Angeles was not signifi-
cantly affected by this law, since almost all of the attorneys
in town had gone east to fight for the Confederacy. Only Colonel Kewen remained, and he spent most of his time in Sacramento.[8]

Two months later, in June, the legislature demanded a for-
mal profession of loyalty from California teachers. This
teachers' oath of allegiance created a stir in Los Angeles and
caused a serious disruption in the schools. Several teachers
refused to sign and resigned their positions. Two instructors
with more sturdy backbone, Mrs. Thomas Foster and William
McKee, ignored the oath and continued to teach. The Los
Angeles Board of Education refused to punish the recalci-
trants and was charged with indifference to the loyalty or
disloyalty of its teachers. Nevertheless, most of the city's
teachers did sign the oath. They soon found themselves with
few pupils, as parents who were Southern sympathizers refused to have their offspring taught by Unionists. School at-
tendance fell off until, in 1865, the census showed only 331
out of 1,009 children of school age attending public institutions. The remainder were about equally divided between
private schools and the streets.[9]

As the summer of 1863 approached, momentous news from
the war fronts engaged the attention of Angelenos. General
Grant was laying siege to Vicksburg, but the Confederate
defenders gave every indication of holding out indefinitely.
In the East, the Union disaster at Chancellorsville was given
front page coverage by the *Star*, as were rumors of peace. The
Star printed a long speech by Richard O'Gorman of New
York, entitled "The Folly of Civil War." As June ended, the
Star, flaunting its Confederate sympathies, announced "Glo-

[7] Harold M. Hyman, "New Light on Cohen v. Wright: California's First
Loyalty Oath Case," *P. H. R.*, May 1959. Hyman touches on the application of
loyalty oaths in Civil War California, a subject in need of more thorough study.
[8] Robinson, p. 48.
[9] Newmark, p. 321; Walters, p. 45; Willard, p. 303.

rious News!" General Lee had crossed the Potomac and was marching north—"Highly encouraging" Hamilton thought. Not mentioned was a little town in Pennsylvania, Gettysburg by name, where two great armies were about the decide the fate of the Union.[10]

[10] *Star*, May 23, June 13 and 27, 1863.

HIGH TIDE

THE FOURTH OF JULY, 1863, was observed in subdued fashion
in Los Angeles. Sectional feeling was too bitter for any open
celebration by the Union faithful. There were picnics and
social gatherings, and a few fireworks were heard during the
evening. Staunch Unionists journeyed south to Drum Barracks, where the California Volunteers celebrated the day
with the usual dress parade, martial music, and patriotic
orations.[1]

The *Star* voiced no objections to the quiet observance of
the Fourth in Los Angeles, but was highly critical of the festivities in San Francisco. The celebration there was denounced as "a petty party triumph . . . wanting in patriotism
. . . instead of the celebration of a glorious event, the Declaration of Independence . . . there was the vile wretch Swett, of
infamous amalgamation notoriety, reading Lincoln's abolition proclamation." John Swett was State Superintendent of
Public Education. His crime, in the eyes of Hamilton, was
not only that he was a Union supporter, but—far worse—he
favored educating Negro children.[2]

War news filtered into Los Angeles via telegraph and, at
last, loyal citizens had something really to cheer about. The

    [1] *Star*, July 4, 1863; Newmark, p. 321. Newmark writes that the 4th of July
military celebration was at Camp Latham, but he is certainly mistaken. Camp
Latham was abandoned the previous October.
    [2] *Star*, July 18, 1863.

Star at first adopted a wait-and-see stance regarding "sensational rumors" of Union victories at Vicksburg and Gettysburg. But in a few days it became obvious to the most partisan Southern supporter that the Confederacy had suffered grievous defeats. As Unionists in town celebrated the glorious Northern victories, the temperament of local secessionists became foul and threatening. After the lives of several loyal celebrants were allegedly threatened, United States Marshal Henry D. Barrows dispatched an urgent call for help to Colonel James F. Curtis, the new commandant at Drum Barracks. On July 31st, a detachment of infantry, 100 strong, from Drum Barracks marched into Los Angeles and set up camp on the east bank of the Los Angeles River. The *News*, obviously relieved, stated, "They will be stationed in this vicinity for some time, and it will be well for 'unruly persons' to be a little quiet, especially when Union rejoicings take place."[3] The troops remained in town until mid-September, then, with quiet at least temporarily restored, they returned to Drum Barracks.

California Democrats made an attempt to reunite the party as the 1863 political campaign got under way. Meeting in Sacramento in July, the Democrats nominated John G. Downey, the former governor and Los Angeles citizen, for the governorship. Los Angeles County Democrats assembled the following month and voiced strong support for Downey, the "peace" candidate, and the party platform supporting "The Constitution as it is, the Union as it was." Colonel Kewen and Ignacio Sepúlveda were renominated for the assembly and, as a reward for his long and steadfast service to the party, Henry Hamilton of the *Star* was selected for the state senate nomination.[4]

The Union Party nominated Frederick F. Low, San Francisco and Marysville banker, for governor. Local candidates

---

[3] *Tri-Weekly News*, August 3, 1863; Newmark, p. 321.
[4] *Star*, July 18, August 8, 1863.

included Francisco P. Ramírez, former editor of the Spanish-language newspaper *El Clamor Público*, for the state senate and Manuel Garfias and David Lewis for assembly.

The September election was hotly contested by both parties. Although Low and the Union Party were victorious state-wide, the Democrats won again in Los Angeles County. But the margin of victory was narrow, a fact the *Star* attributed to unscrupulous methods of the military: "At a public meeting held here on Sunday evening prior to the election the principal speakers were military officers, who were coarse and malignant in their denunciations of the various Democratic candidates. At some precincts in the county, the military were stationed; at others they rode up during the hours of election; in this city a detachment of dragoons were drawn up and halted in front of the polls, whilst the military band paraded the town all day, informing us, in the most insinuating manner, that John Brown's soul was still marching on." Hamilton blamed the state-wide victory of Low and the Union Party on demagogury, threats, intimidation, misrepresentation, and pilferings, and further stated that "On no former occasion was the weight of civil and military, of State and Federal influence, so authoratively exercised, or so shamelessly abused." He added that the Democratic Party was "in no ways disheartened by this defeat." [5]

The *News*, in discussing the election results, attributed the Democratic decline to Hamilton's being on the ticket. It denied the charge of corruption made by the *Star*, alleging instead that the local secessionists had stuffed the ballot boxes. [6]

The vote for governor in Los Angeles city and county was as follows:

	Los Angeles City	Los Angeles County
John G. Downey	426	982
Frederick F. Low	332	702

[5] *Star*, September 5 and 12, 1863.
[6] *News*, September 7, 1863.

Henry Hamilton was elected to the state senate and both Democrats, Kewen and Sepúlveda, won the assembly race.

With the election over, and before leaving for Sacramento to take his seat in the state senate, Hamilton stepped up his attacks on President Lincoln. He was incensed, he said, to constantly hear that the president was honest: "We hear it stated continually by those misguided men who believe in God and Abraham Lincoln that, 'Old Abe is honest, if nothing else.' . . . No greater fallacy than this ever found lodgment in the brains of sensible men. Abe Lincoln honest! Why, his every act, from the hour of his departure from Springfield to Washington to begin his saturnalia of blood, till the present day, has been replete with gross and palpable deception. If a single honest action has characterized his administrative policy since he assumed the reins of power, we confess to an entire ignorance of it."[7]

In late November, 1863, Hamilton left for the state capital on the northbound stage. Before leaving, he appointed F. G. J. Margetson to manage the *Star* during his absence. The new editor, an anti-administration Democrat with views little different from Hamilton's, continued the *Star's* attacks on Lincoln and Unionists in general.

Meantime, Hamilton's opponent in the recent election, Francisco P. Ramírez, filed notice of his intention to contest the election with the clerk of the district court. Ramírez's arguments were that Hamilton was disloyal to the United States and was not a citizen. The defeated Union candidate also charged corruption at the polls. The *News* supported Ramírez's claims and suggested that Hamilton deserved a seat at Alcatraz instead of Sacramento. And, the newspaper inquired, where were the Irishman's naturalization papers. Hamilton's disloyalty, the *News* continued, was a proven fact; he had tried to provoke rebellion in Los Angeles by printing

[7] *Star*, November 7, 1863.

"incendiary articles" which in any other country would have resulted in his incarceration or execution.[8]

The district court appointed two local justices of the peace as commissioners to investigate Ramírez's charges against Hamilton. Numerous witnesses were called to testify and much evidence was accumulated. The results of the investigation were sent to Sacramento and presented to the Senate Committee on Elections. Evidently most of the testimony collected in Los Angeles was favorable to Hamilton; the Senate Committee failed to establish proof of the editor's disloyalty, found no conclusive evidence of election irregularities, and declared Ramírez's claims were not established. The committee did not investigate whether Hamilton was still a citizen of Ireland; it was later found that he had been naturalized in 1856. The committee report was submitted to the state senate, which thereupon concurred in the opinion of the committee and dismissed Ramírez's petition. Henry Hamilton kept his seat as senator from Los Angeles County.[9]

Hamilton's six-month career as a state senator was undistinguished. He served on several standing committees, including those dealing with public printing and commerce and navigation. He submitted a few minor bills, mostly dealing with minor local issues, and voted regularly on the rest. He was known to his senate colleagues as one of the "five Copperheads" and, because of his anti-Union stand on many issues, was usually at odds with the majority.[10]

The specter of crime and violence cast an ugly pall over Los Angeles during the final weeks of 1863. The spree began on November 15th, when, not far from town, a lone miner named R. A. Hester was brutally murdered by a border ruf-

[8] *News*, September 25 and 28, November 18, December 4 and 23, 1863.
[9] "Report of the Senate Committee on Elections in the Contested Election Case: Ramirez vs. Hamilton," *Appendix to Journals of Senate and Assembly of the Fifteenth Session* . . . (Sacramento, 1864), II, Nos. 11, 12, cited by Rice, p. 248–249.
[10] Rice, p. 250.

fian known as Boston Daimwood, while several of the latter's
cohorts stood by to prevent interference. Daimwood then
boasted to terrified onlookers that he intended to "pay his respects," supposedly in like manner, to a number of other Los
Angeles citizens. The news of the crime reached Los Angeles
fast, and within hours a sheriff's posse and vigilante group
were in hot pursuit of the murderous band. Daimwood and
three of his fellow thugs were captured and lodged in jail to
await trial. But many local citizens felt that the slow course
of justice was too good for these bullying killers, and a vigilante group was hastily organized. On November 21st, over
200 armed vigilantes marched to the county jail and demanded the keys from Tomás Sánchez, the sheriff. When he
refused to accede to their demands, the mob broke down the
jail doors, seized the four scoundrels and hanged them to the
portico of the old City Hall on Spring Street. Sheriff Sánchez
threatened to arrest the vigilante leaders; but so strong was
public sentiment, as reflected in the newspapers, in support
of the summary executions, that no legal action was taken.[11]

An interesting sidelight, and good illustration of the char-
acter of mob psychology, occurred during the lynching. As
the criminals were in the process of being executed, the clat-
tering of horses' hoofs was heard and the cry was raised that
cavalry from Drum Barracks was fast approaching to rescue
the prisoners. Instantly the vigilantes and their supporters
scurried for cover in all directions. Instead of soldiers, however, the horsemen proved to be a contingent of El Monte
boys, coming to assist in the necktie party.[12]

The innate evil of justice, vigilante style, was made apparent by an incident that occurred during the course of the
seizure and execution of the Daimwood gang. There was a
fifth prisoner in the jail that day, a teenage boy named Wood,
whose offense was no worse than the theft of some chickens.

[11] *Star*, November 28, 1863; Newmark, p. 324.
[12] Newmark, p. 324.

The mob, upon finding the lad in confinement with the four murderers, determined that, while they were at it, the jail might as well be cleared of all malefactors. They decided to kill him, too. He was led outside with the other prisoners, and ordered to climb upon a large empty case so that the noose hanging from the rafters of the City Hall portico could be placed around his neck. Harris Newmark related what happened next: "I shall never forget the spectacle of the youth, apparently oblivious of his impending doom, as he placed his hands upon the box and vaulted lightly to the top (just as he might have done at an innocent gymnastic contest), and his parting salutation, 'I'm going to die a game hen-chicken!' The removal of the case a moment later, after the noose had been thrown over and drawn about the lad's head, left the poor victim suspended beyond human aid." [13]

Another vigilante execution occurred two weeks later. Manuel Cerradel had been arrested several months previously and charged with the murder, in November 1862, of John Rains, proprietor of Rancho Cucamonga and well known in Los Angeles. In time, Cerradel was tried and convicted in county court and sentenced to ten years in San Quentin Prison. On December 9th, Sheriff Sánchez, with the prisoner in hand, journeyed to Wilmington and boarded the ferry steamer *Cricket*, to escort Cerradel to the *Senator*, lying at anchor three miles out and about to depart for San Francisco. Also boarding the *Cricket* were a suspiciously large number of other men, apparently taking the harbor voyage as sightseers. Once the little steamer had cleared the estuary, these silent passengers, at a prearranged signal, overpowered Sheriff Sánchez and seized the culprit. Professing themselves indignant at the light sentence imposed, the vigilantes threw a noose around Cerradel's neck and hung him from the flagstaff. When the prisoner was dead, his body was lowered and stones, brought aboard in packages by the vigilantes, who had

[13] *Ibid.*, pp. 324–325.

evidently planned every detail. were tied to his feet. The corpse was then tossed overboard into the harbor waters.[14]

Violence was threatened, but narrowly averted, in Los Angeles with the announcement, in November 1863, that the military draft was about to begin California. J. J. Warner was appointed Deputy Provost Marshal for Los Angeles County, and William L. Reynolds Enrolling Officer, for the purpose of registering all able-bodied citizens for possible military service. Immediately there was an angry outburst by Southern sympathizers in town. With violence apparently imminent, two companies of California Volunteers from Drum Barracks hurried to Los Angeles and were quartered on the outskirts of town. Following further disturbances that threatened to turn into general rioting, one company of soldiers encamped in the Plaza, while a squad of armed troopers guarded Warner's office. Needless to say, J. J. Warner was a very unpopular man about town during this period, particularly among the large and highly vociferous secessionist element. According to Harris Newmark, had it not been for the presence of soldiers from Drum Barracks, "this first step toward compusory enrollment would have undoubtedly resulted in riotous disturbances." In time, the unrest over the draft died down, as no one was actually conscripted for military service in California. Volunteers filled the state's quota.[15]

[14] *Ibid.*, p. 326.
[15] Newmark, p. 323; Thompson and West, p. 97; Rice, p. 244.

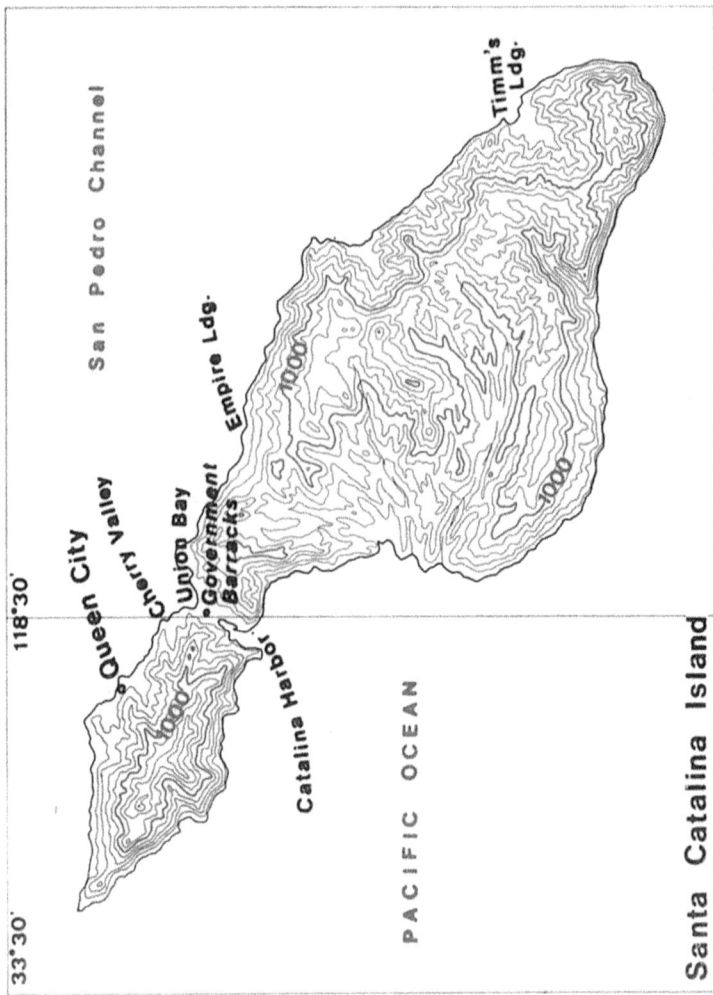

Santa Catalina Island

ECONOMIC WOES

ON NEW YEAR'S DAY, 1864, a detachment of California Volunteers from Drum Barracks steamed across the San Pedro Channel to take possession of Santa Catalina Island. The following day, a temporary military camp was set up near the Isthmus, and soon thereafter the island was fortified with a twelve-pound gun, the only piece of coast artillery near Los Angeles at the time. Captain Benjamin R. West, army commander on the island, in accordance with instructions from General Wright, issued the following order to inhabitants: "I hereby notify all persons on Catalina Island to leave the same before the first of February next."[1]

The army occupation of Santa Catalina, along with the preemptory command for all persons—mostly gold miners—to leave the island, set in motion wild rumors and speculation that have lasted into recent times.

Prospectors had been scouring the hills of western Catalina since April, 1863, when "very rich mines" of gold were reported on the island. First to locate claims were Martin Kimberly and Daniel Way, with their Mammoth Lead, near the Isthmus, and St. Nicholas Lead in Cherry Valley. A rush of eager miners invested the island and the San Pedro Mining District was formed, its boundaries to embrace "all the Is-

---

[1] O.R., Ser. I, Vol. L, Pt. 2, pp. 714, 718, 720; see also Adelaide LeMert Doran, *The Ranch that Was Robbins': Santa Catalina Island, California* (Los Angeles: privately printed, 1964), pp. 78–79.

lands of Los Angeles County and the Coast Range of mountains between the northern and southern boundaries of the County of Los Angeles." A crude mining metropolis, Queen City, was staked out at Wilson's Harbor. Ore taken from the island mines reportedly assayed at $85 to $150 to the ton in San Francisco.[2]

The mining boom on Catalina was abruptly cut short by the military takeover. The army's active interest in the island was first manifested in November 1863, when Major Henry Hancock and a small detachment of soldiers from Drum Barracks surveyed Santa Catalina and declared it suitable for a military station. Shortly after receiving Hancock's report, General Wright ordered the military occupation of the island and the removal of civilian inhabitants. Unfortunately, the army never announced the reason for the takeover, thereby setting in motion a web of intriguing speculation.

Angelenos received first notice of the occupation by reading a short announcement in the *Los Angeles Tri-Weekly News* on December 28th, signed by Captain West, which gave no reason for the army's action but merely directed all persons on the island to leave by the February 1st deadline. In its next issue, December 30th, the *News* editorialized on the seizure. The reason for the occupation was two-fold, thought the newspaper: The island would be a convenient place to detain traitors, and the army stationed there would "flustrate [sic] some evil design. . . . Rebel emissaries are running at large everywhere among us." A week later, the *News* elaborated on the supposed Confederate designs on Santa Catalina, implying that the island miners were secessionists and stating that the army would most likely take over the "rebel deposits" [mines]. Still later, the newspaper alleged that the military forces on the island would protect commerce—probably

---

[2] Doran, pp. 78–84; Robinson, *The Island of Santa Catalina* (Los Angeles: Title Guarantee & Trust Co., 1941), unpaged.

meaning the protection of merchant ships from Confederate privateers, although this was not specifically stated.[3]

The real reason for the military occupation of Santa Catalina had nothing to do with alleged Confederate plots. In actuality, the Department of the Pacific wanted to use the island as an Indian reservation. The Klamath, Redwood, and Trinity Indians of the Humboldt District, in northwestern California, had for some time been in a state of unrest and would not remain on their army-designated reservations. General Wright concluded that the best solution was to remove the Indians from this northwest corner of the state and relocate them far from their homeland. As a new location for the troublesome Indians, Wright suggested Santa Catalina. In listing the island's assets, he mentioned the benefits of ample wood and water, good land for farming, a fine harbor, much pasturage, and abundant fish. "With all of these advantages I consider it the most eligible location for an Indian reservation that can be found on this coast."[4] The General then requested that the War Department and the Department of the Interior allow him to go ahead with his colonization plan.

Meantime, the false rumors of Confederate designs on the island continued to circulate. The reason for General Wright's refusal to make any public announcement as to his real plan for Catalina is easy to determine. There would have been consternation in southern California had it been known that the army wanted to colonize the nearby island with hostile Indians recently on the warpath. To prevent additional unrest in an area of the state already upset with the course of the war and largely hostile to the Union government, local citizens were never told the truth.

[3] *News*, January 6 and 29, 1864.
[4] *O.R.*, Ser. I, Vol. L, Pt. 2, p. 706. See Theodore Kornweibel, Jr., "The Occupation of Santa Catalina During the Civil War," *C.H.S. Quarterly*, December 1967.

In the end, General Wright's Indian colonization plan came to naught. A lack of enthusiasm on the part of the War Department and adverse decisions by the Department of the Interior combined to defeat the scheme. Santa Catalina was swiftly evacuated by the army once it became certain that the Indian reservation would not be located there. On September 14, 1864, the last of the "army of occupation" left the island. A few of the evicted miners returned, but the gold boom was over and Santa Catalina slumbered for two decades. But the myth of Confederate designs on the island did not slumber. Revived by Los Angeles historian J. M. Guinn, given currency by Harris Newmark, William Spaulding, and even W. W. Robinson, it still survives to distort the history of southern California during the Civil War.[5]

Eighteen hundred sixty-four was a bad year for southern California. A stifling drought hung heavy over the land, with disastrous consequences for the cattleman and farmer. Since the heavy downpour of January 1862, scarcely a drop of rain had fallen on the plains around Los Angeles, "withering every remnant of vegetation and leaving not a green spot on the whole plain. The hills are now as red and arid as we ever saw them," wrote the *Star*. "In passing over the plains, it is sad to see the number of dead cattle; while those that survive, present an appearance, such as to produce sympathy for the sufferings of the poor dumb animals." A month later, the *Star* sadly reported, "All indications of rain seem to have passed away, leaving the prospects of the farmer utterly hopeless." To make matters even worse, the late spring brought scorch-

[5] Kornweibel, p. 345. For perpetuation of the Catalina Confederate myth, see J. M. Guinn, "The Lost Mines of Santa Catalina," *Annual Publications of H.S. S.C.*, 1912–1913, pp. 43–48; Newmark, p. 318; William A. Spalding, *History and Reminiscences: Los Angeles City and County, California* (Los Angeles: J. R. Finnell & Sons, 1931), p. 163; Robinson, *Island of Catalina*. Aurora Hunt, in her *Army of the Pacific*, pp. 248–250, correctly states that Wright desired to colonize the Humboldt Indians on the island. Kornweibel is severely critical of local historians in general, and calls Catalina "a case in point of the frequent inadequacy of local history which is no more than uncritical repetition of earlier works brought up to date."

ing Santa Ana winds from the desert, resulting in "dense clouds of stifling dust that filled the air, and dimmed the light of the sun, and blinded and choked people." Ranchers like Abel Stearns suffered grievous economic loss; thousands of his cattle lay dead and dying over his vast ranchos, while most of the remainder of his starving animals were slaughtered for the trifling value of their hides and horns. The carcasses of dead cattle lay strewn about the parched water holes and alongside streams from which every trace of moisture had disappeared. A drover described the twenty miles of once rich grazing country between Los Angeles and Wilmington as "a regular mass of dead cattle." The *News* painted a despairing picture of the great ranchos around Los Angeles: "Thousands of carcasses strew the plains in all directions, a short distance from this city, and the sight is harrowing in the extreme. We believe the stock interest of this county, as well as the adjoining counties, to be 'played out' entirely. Famine has done its work, and nothing can now save what few cattle remain on the desert California ranches." [6]

It is difficult to estimate just how many cattle perished in the great drought of 1862–1864, or were slaughtered by the ranchers for the minute salvage value of their hides and horns. The only definite figures available are the federal census returns for 1860 and 1870, which reveal that the number of cattle in Los Angeles County fell from 70,000 to 20,000 —a loss of over 71 per cent. [7] Along with the dead livestock were ranchers and businessmen economically ruined. In 1863 and 1864, property values in the county declined drastically, range lands assessed as low as 10 cents an acre. The landowners were so hard pressed for ready cash that taxes on at least five-sixths of the property were allowed to become delinquent. Land once valuable was picked up by speculators for the merest song.

[6] *Star*, January 23, March 17, April 9, 1864; *News*, January 22 and March 9, 1864; Newmark, pp. 328–329; Robert Glass Cleland, *The Cattle on a Thousand Hills* (San Marino: The Huntington Library, 1964), pp. 130–131, 134–137.

The ranchers' woes had a rippling effect on the entire southern California economy. The Los Angeles merchants suffered through a severe business recession that Harris New-mark described as the worst in his 65 years in the city. The long-time merchant recalled, "With a total assessment of something like two million dollars in the County, not a cent of taxes (at least in the city) was collected. Men were so miserably poor that confidence mutually weakened, and merchants refused to trust those who, as land and cattle-barons, but a short time before had been so influential. . . . How great was the depreciation in values may be seen from the fact that notes given by Francis Temple, and bearing heavy interest, were peddled about at fifty cents on the dollar and even then found few purchasers."[8]

The age of "The Cattle on a Thousand Hills" was over in southern California. "But out of the drastic losses inflicted by the Great Drought," writes Robert Glass Cleland, "came a new economic order. Forbidding heaps of bones and skeletons, everywhere bleaching in the sun, symbolized the ruin of the universal industry of southern California. Thereafter, the 'cow counties' lost their distinctive appellation. The day of unfenced ranchos, of enormous herds of half-wild cattle, of manorial estates, and pleasure-loving *paisanos* came to its inevitable close. But, in its passing, something of color and romance faded forever from the California scene."[9]

A source of much economic discontent in Los Angeles, as well as throughout the state during the Civil War years, was the use of legal tender notes or "greenbacks." When the war broke out the United States Treasury was practically devoid of hard currency to finance the Union military effort. The government resorted to the issuing of greenbacks as legal ten-der, provoking considerable opposition at first. But the plea of "absolute necessity" silenced most of the complaints, and it

[7] Cleland, *Cattle*, p. 135.
[8] Newmark, p. 328.
[9] Cleland, *Cattle*, p. 137.

was not long until most of the population of the Northern states became reconciled to the measure. However, legal tender notes were never well received in California, even among the loyal populace. Gold had long been the main staple commodity of the state, and many of California's business leaders predicted monetary devaluation and financial depression if greenbacks replaced specie. San Francisco merchants were almost united in opposition to paper currency, and made strenuous attempts to maintain the prevailing gold and silver money. A judgment of the state supreme court in 1862 ruling that the notes could not be used in paying taxes heartened the dissenters, as did the Specific Contract Act, passed by the state legislature the following year. This act allowed contracting parties to specify whether a debt should be paid in coin or legal tender notes. An attempt by Union loyalists to abrogate the Specific Contract Act was made in the 1863–1864 legislative session. Loyalty clashed with economic self-interest, and the latter won—the act remained on the books.[10]

Los Angeles merchants were as strongly opposed to the use of greenbacks as were the businessmen of San Francisco. The *Star* called the notes almost worthless and related how local storekeepers were loath to accept them: "... it requires a cartload of them to pay for a plug of tobacco or a drink." Harris Newmark stated that, at one time during the war, legal tender notes shrank to but 35 cents to the dollar in local exchange, and one seldom could recover more than 65 or 75 cents to the dollar. The *News*, in line with its Union sentiments, supported the use of legal tender notes, but readily accepted advertisements from local shopkeepers airing their grievances against the paper money. Los Angeles brewery owner J. Murat placed a notice in the *News* protesting the action of one John Jones, who had used greenbacks to pay for a large order of beer and yeast; "I merely insert this," declared the

[10] Ellison, pp. 208–230, has a comprehensive discussion of the legal tender issue as it affected California. See also Rice, pp. 244–245.

disgusted Murat, "to show how well Mr. John Jones likes to drink lager beer and eat bread . . . but does not like so well to pay for the same." Some San Francisco merchants realized fortunes when greenback devaluation occurred, as they bought their merchandise in the East with paper currency and sold it on the West Coast for gold. Angelenos enjoyed no such benefit and were practically at the mercy of the northern city; they purchased most of their wares in San Francisco with gold, and were therefore obliged to liquidate in specie to realize a profit.[11] This problem, coupled with the economic depression caused largely by the two-year drought, made Los Angeles merchants an unhappy lot during the final years of the Civil War.

The economic problems of southern California in the mid-1860s may have resulted in inconvenience and financial hardship for the Anglo merchants and land owners, but they proved an absolute disaster to the Spanish-speaking citizenry. All but a few of the great Californio land-owning families were plunged into debt from which they did not recover, being eventually forced to sell their ranchos at far below market value to satisfy creditors. And, as is invariably the case in any economic depression, it was the poor who suffered most. The long drought and economic stagnation destroyed the basic livelihood of the poor Californios, cattle raising and farming, forcing many of them into abject poverty. Henry D. Barrows, observing the sad plight of these local Mexican-Americans, wrote in May 1864, "Business is dull and times are exceedingly hard. Much suffering and destitution among the poorer classes of the population in this part of the state are anticipated before another rainy season comes around. Hitherto the lower class of Mexicans, when worst came to worst, could steal beef rather than starve; but most of the cattle have died off, or have been driven away, and there are very few left for them to steal. Ordinarily they might make a shift to live on

---

[11] Newmark, p. 319; Rice, p. 245; *Star*, January 17, 1863; *News*, August 4, 1864.

atole, frijoles, pumpkins, etc., but many poor families have not even their animals left them with which to plow. . . . Serious fears are entertained that many *pobres* will have to starve this season or be dependent on charity for the wherewithal to sustain life." Social historian Leonard Pitt, in discussing the Californios' plight of 1862–1864, observes that "they suffered a physical disaster as great as if they stood in the path of Sherman's march to the sea."[12]

[12] Leonard Pitt, *The Decline of the Californios: A Social History of the Spanish-Speaking Californians, 1846–1890* (Berkeley, University of California Press, 1970), p. 244. The Barrows quote is from the *San Francisco Bulletin*, May 5, 1864.

THE GRIMNESS OF WAR

THE CIVIL WAR entered its most terrible phase as the months
of spring gave way to summer, 1864. The grim realities of
human carnage were hammered home, week after week, on
the pages of the *Star* and the *News*. The armies of Grant and
Lee were locked in a relentless slugging match, and the casu-
alty lists mounted fearfully on both sides. Virginia was liter-
ally drenched in blood. Even staunch Union supporters wondered if the slaughter would ever end, and whether victory
was possible.

The *Star* expressed horror at the national bloodbath, and
placed the blame squarely on the shoulders of Abraham Lincoln, that "imbecile tyrant" in the White House. "And for
what?" asked the *Star*; "The political and social institutions
of a continent have been revolutionized to vindicate the ir-
rational and divinely refuted theory of the Equality of Races,
and to invest the African—stamped by the hand of Omnipo-
tence with the irradicable brand of servility, with the perfect
political and social equality with the Caucasian. For this has
our national unity been destroyed; for this, the Constitution
has been obliterated; for this, our liberties subverted; for
this, the Continent has been plunged into war, and baptised
in blood; and for this, and this alone, must untold thousands
of brave men lay down their lives."[1]

[1] *Star*, January 16, 1864.

As never before, Henry Hamilton revealed his hatred of Lincoln, the Union Administration and, most of all, Negroes. When news reached Los Angeles of the Fort Pillow Massacre, where Confederates under General Forrest executed all captured Union Negro troops, the *Star* rejoiced: "It is all very well for negro troops to cut the throats of the helpless women and children of the South . . . but if they happen to be caught in the act of thus 'serving their country's cause' and get their brains blown out or their carcasses pinned down with avenging bayonets, they are [called] victims of Southern brutality . . . We suggest to our 'loyal' friends that if they cannot endure to have their colored brethren killed, they had better keep them out of the army."[2]

The threat of conscription once again disturbed Angelenos in April, 1864, when General Wright announced that ten more regiments were to be raised in the Pacific states. The town was "in perfect ferment" over the proposed draft, said the *Star*, and it would require 15,000 troops here to enforce it among an unwilling populace: "We presume that the recruiting offices will be opened in a few days, but it may be set down as next to a novel certainty that they will have to be closed again before the regiments are filled . . . those who clamor for a vigorous prosecution of the war . . . would sooner hear the devil roar than a drum beat . . . the attempt to raise troops by conscription here will prove about as effectual as would an effort to boil water with a seive. . . . It is downright nonsense to talk about enforcing a conscription from a population of which one half are totally opposed to the war and all the purposes for which it is conducted, and the other half quite as bitterly opposed to *fighting*, however much they may be in favor of the War." The *News* reported "a flock of skedaddlers" had hurriedly left town to avoid being drafted. The excitement died down in a few weeks; the army received enough volunteers—mostly from northern California—to fill

[2] *Star*, April 23, 1864.

its new regiments, and the conscription offices never opened in Los Angeles.[3]

As local unrest mounted over the news of stark horror on the eastern battlefields, Union authorities in Los Angeles became increasingly vigilant. Persons were arrested for allegedly uttering disloyal sentiments. In May, a J. F. Bilderbeck was placed under arrest and conveyed to Drum Barracks, charged with publicly stating that he hoped the Confederates would "kill every negro who might be taken with arms in his hands, and every white man who might be in command of them or with them." A few weeks later, "Nigger Pete" Biggs, Los Angeles barber, vociferously proclaimed his attachment to the cause of the Confederacy, whereupon he was taken into custody and escorted to Drum Barracks. According to Harris Newmark, this colorful Negro ex-slave with his odd loyalty to the forces of slavery was made to foot it, with iron chain and ball attached to his ankle, all the way from Los Angeles to Wilmington. Enroute, an unchastised "Nigger Pete" threw his hat in the air and gave three whoops for Jeff Davis as he passed some acquaintances on the road, thereby compounding his "crime." Neither Bilderbeck nor "Nigger Pete" was held long in confinement. Colonel James F. Curtis, Drum Barracks commandant, released both men upon their signing an oath of allegiance.[4]

The *Star* claimed outrageous interference in the city election of May 3rd, when Democrat Damien Marchessault was reelected mayor of Los Angeles over Union candidate John G. Nichols by a margin of only eight votes. The closeness of the vote, according to the *Star*, was the result of soldiers from Drum Barracks who "in a military manner marched to the polls, thence in single file to the ballot box, and there deposited the vote which had been placed in their hands by the commanding officer."[5]

[3] *Star*, April 2 and 16, 1864; *News*, April 1 and 6, 1864.
[4] *Star*, May 14, 1864; *News*, May 10, 1864; Newmark, pp. 330–331.
[5] *Star*, May 7, 1864.

Early in July, 1864, Major General Irwin McDowell, fresh from failure on the eastern battlefronts, arrived in San Francisco to take over command of the Army's Department of the Pacific from aging Brigadier General George Wright. Ultra-loyalists in California had long been unhappy with Wright for allegedly catering to the secessionists by his refusal to adopt harsh measures against persons accused of disloyalty. These super-Unionists had several times petitioned the War Department for Wright's removal, and their desires had at last been heeded. General Wright, in a farewell letter addressed to the people of California, hinted at the reason for his removal: "Had I for a moment yielded to the insane demands of a radical press and its co-laborers, I should have filled my forts with political prisoners to gratify personal hatred, causing such an outburst of indignation at such a course as to render it almost certain that civil war and bloodshed would have followed." [6]

In Los Angeles, the *Star* praised General Wright for his moderate policies and blamed his removal on "Jacobin leaders." The *News*, however, was glad to see the old general go. Piqued at Wright's criticism of the radical press, the *News* published a reprint from the *Marysville Appeal*: "The old granny with patriotic buttons on his coat, who has been favored with distinction by the government out of respect for his gray hairs, publishes a farewell address to the people of this state. We are so well pleased with the announcement of his retirement that our wrath at its unwarranted language is more than appeased. His allusion to the radical press is a direct insult to every Union paper in the state, although only intended for those who have been outspoken in favor of his removal. . . . But we in common with Union papers feel in good humor at the retirement of General Wright, old fuss and feathers, to be too severe. We are willing to attach all his

[6] Bancroft, Vol. VII, p. 471. See also Ellison, p. 203; and Hunt, *Army of the Pacific*, pp. 349–350.

faults to the ravages of time and not to any fault of the old man's heart. He departs and as we say good bye forever, sink all ill will and thoughts of his short comings."[7]

General Wright remained in San Francisco, serving under McDowell, for almost a year. In 1865 he was assigned to command the Department of Oregon, but he never reached his new post. Enroute from San Francisco to the Columbia River, he perished in the wreck of the steamer *Brother Jonathan,* having served with honor, if not great distinction, the army on the Pacific Coast for twelve years.[8]

Mention should be made of an elaborate and fanciful scheme, unknown to Union authorities until Confederate records were seized after the war, to raise an army of Southern partisans in California for the reconquest of Arizona and New Mexico. The concocter of this plot was "Judge" Lansford W. Hastings, a native of Ohio who had lived in California for over twenty years. Hastings had authored a handbook on the overland trail for use by emigrants, had been an associate of Sutter before the gold discovery, and had been involved in the writing of the first California constitution. More recently, he had practiced law and held a judgeship in northern California. There is nothing in his known career to explain why he had become a secret, active Confederate sympathizer.

In September 1863, Hastings presented himself at the Shreveport, Louisiana, headquarters of General Kirby Smith, commander of all Confederate forces west of the Mississippi River. Before the surprised Southern general, Hastings outlined his scheme to seize the Southwest for the Confederacy. He would return to California via Guaymas, Mexico, and from Los Angeles organize a secret force of 3,000 to 5,000 secessionists, disguised as miners. He would be aided in this

---

[7] *Star,* April 16, 1864; *News,* July 19, 1864, cited in Hunt, *Army of the Pacific,* pp. 349–350.
[8] Bancroft, Vol. VII, p. 471.

effort by "secret organizations," presumably the Knights of the Golden Circle and/or the Knights of the Columbian Star. Once organized, his pseudo-miners would cross the desert in small groups so as not to attract the attention of Union authorities and rendezvous near the Colorado River. Once his force was gathered along the river, he would pounce on Fort Yuma, capture it and release the Confederate prisoners held there. Meanwhile, another group, also disguised as miners, would take ship from San Pedro to Guaymas and march overland to rendezvous with the main force near Fort Yuma. The combined expedition would then launch an all-out attack on Fort Buchanan in southern Arizona and move eastward to the Rio Grande and El Paso, where they would meet the Confederate army in Texas. To maintain Confederate control of the Southwest, Hastings asserted, "I can raise in California from three thousand to ten thousand superior troops, and every six months I can throw an additional force into Arizona from California during this unholy war." He concluded his presentation to General Smith by asking that the Confederate government supply him with sufficient funds to carry out his plan.

General Smith was noncommittal about Hastings' fantastic scheme, but he gave the latter a letter of introduction to the Confederate Secretary of War, James Seddon, and sent him to Richmond. Seddon expressed interest in Hastings' plan but, as the Californian was a stranger to him and was without military experience, reserved his judgment. In November 1863, General Smith, to whom Seddon had sent Hastings' proposal for detailed consideration, replied that "Judge Hastings has wholly failed to satisfy me as to the propriety of trusting him in so important a matter . . . and [I]cannot in any event . . . furnish the necessary funds."

Jefferson Davis was appraised of the scheme, but after ten days' consideration of the project referred it back to his Secretary of War, who reported against it. But Hastings was not a man to give up easily, and he submitted another plan to Davis. He scaled down his proposed force to 1,500 men and stated he would put it in operation "without the financial support of the Confederacy," if only its president would promise reimbursement in the event of its success.

Hastings' scheme promised such dividends, and the possibility of recruiting a pro-Confederate force in southern California seemed so plausible, at least from Richmond's point of view, that President Davis finally agreed to try it. On February 4, 1864, Secretary of War Seddon handed Hastings a letter of instructions to be hand-carried to Kirby Smith. According to the letter, Hastings was commissioned a major in the Confederate Army and was authorized to raise troops in southern California for the seizure and occupation of Arizona. General Smith was directed to raise the necessary funds —$10,000 to $12,000—by the sale of cotton in Mexico. Hastings and a disbursing officer appointed by General Smith would proceed at once to the port in Mexico to which recruits from California would be directed. Then Hastings would continue secretly to Los Angeles to set the plan in operation.

With this letter (which was found after the war in Confederate files), Lansford W. Hastings and his incredible plot disappear from history. There is no solid evidence as to whether or not he returned to California, although one historian has speculated that he probably reached San Francisco in late March or April, 1864. By this time, the Confederacy was in dire straits and faced far more pressing problems than the recapture of the Southwest. Logic suggests that the plan was dropped. Southern California historian Percival J. Cooney writes, "It is probably fortunate for California and Arizona that his mission was deferred until 1864, for, if he had arrived in Richmond earlier in the war, when the Confederacy was in the first flush of its early successes, his plan might have been adopted and history for southern California and Arizona might have had to be written very differently."[9]

[9] Cooney, pp. 63–65. For more on the Hastings plot see Clarence C. Clendenen, "A Confederate Spy in California: A Curious Incident of the Civil War," *Southern California Quarterly*, September 1963; and James A. B. Scherer, *Thirty-first Star* (New York: G. P. Putnam's Sons, 1942), pp. 271–283. Clendenen believes that Hastings returned to California in late March or April, 1864.

WE ARE COMING, FATHER ABRAHAM

PRESIDENT LINCOLN's renomination in June heralded the beginning of the 1864 campaign. As the long days of summer wore on, neither side showed much enthusiasm. The *Star*, apparently resigned to Democratic defeat, initially called the president's reelection a "foregone conclusion." For once, the *News* agreed with Hamilton: The Confederacy, it stated, had come into existence with the election of Lincoln, and it was only fitting that it should expire with the same man in the White House.[1]

As General Grant's army bogged down in the tangled thickets of Virginia, apparently with victory still beyond grasp, the president's fortunes appeared to ebb, while Democratic prospects looked brighter. The *Star* began to exude optimism. In August, Hamilton saw the prospects of Lincoln's reelection "become more clouded every week. . . . His incompetency is forcing itself painfully upon the mere casual observer. . . . The people are becoming disgusted with the prolonged slaughter, and it is probable they will turn the funny old joker out of office."[2]

But Hamilton was deeply worried about the upcoming Democratic National Convention in Chicago. He had heard rumors that General George B. McClellan would be the par-

[1] *Star*, June 11, 1864; *News*, June 14, 1864.
[2] *Star*, August 27, 1864.

ty's standard-bearer. McClellan's nomination would be a fatal mistake, insisted the *Star's* editor. Peace Democrats would not support the general. The term "War Democrat" was a contradiction, he said, "an absurdity—a monstrosity." "We cannot bedieve that the Convention upon which the eyes and prayers of a long suffering people rested could so far betray the sacred trust reposed in it, as to nominate a man whose every antecedent political principle is in direct and violent opposition to the great Party."[3]

One week later, when the news was telegraphed to Los Angeles that the Democrats had chosen McClellan, the *Star* gulped and swallowed the nomination. Below the masthead, the newspaper printed in bold black letters: "For President GEORGE B. MCCLELLAN of Pennsylvania For Vice President GEORGE H. PENDLETON of Ohio." "It is not necessary," the *Star* wrote, "that we should conceal our repugnance to ... McClellan, or affect an enthusiasm we do not feel." But, the paper said, the war must cease and McClellan had accepted the party's peace platform, and this was certainly preferable to Lincoln's war doctrines. Therefore, it declared, Democrats, "in the name of God and humanity," should rally behind the candidate and work for the only peaceable means to dethrone the "corrupt, usurping, bloody-handed despot" now in the White House.[4]

The *News* assaulted McClellan as "the gravedigger of the Chickahominy." It wondered how the Democratic candidate, so recently a war supporter, could thus eat his words without indigestion. His former professions of loyalty, the journal said, contrasted with his recent statements and proved him to be a "false and unscrupulous man."[5]

By late September, Los Angeles was swept into the political whirlwind. The local Democrats joined in a huge rally, fully

[3] *Star*, September 3, 1864; Rice, p. 252.
[4] *Star*, September 10 and 17, 1864.
[5] *News*, September 13, October 1, 1864.

described in the *Star*: "The largest meeting ever held in Los Angeles assembled in front of the Montgomery House on Thursday evening . . . cannon boomed, rockets, tar barrels and other combustibles lit up the heavens, and a splendid band tuned the evening air to harmony. . . . At about seven o'clock, a grand procession, under the direction of Mr. Marchessault, Marshal of the Day, . . . marched all over the city." Speakers included W. G. Dryden, president of the local Democratic Club, John S. Griffin, Benjamin D. Wilson, ex-Governor Downey, and Colonel Edward J. C. Kewen, the latter addressing the mass gathering for an hour "with fervid eloquence and charming rhetoric for which he has been so long justly famed." The crowd carried banners inscribed with sentiments such as "The Union as it was—the Constitution as it is," "McClellan and Pendleton—the only salvation of our country," "There can be no Union without peace," and "States Rights for ever." [6]

Los Angeles Republicans—temporarily allied with "war" Democrats in the National Union Party—made up in enthusiasm what they lacked in numbers. The *News* proclaimed, "Grand Union Rally on Friday Night! Union Men Turn Out! Rally! Rally!" Describing the mass meeting afterwards, the newspaper challenged the *Star*'s assertion that the Democratic rally was larger: "The Union assemblage, held in this city, in front of the Lafayette Hotel . . . was the largest gathering—forming the most extended procession—ever witnessed in Los Angeles or Southern California." The rally began in front of the Lincoln and Johnson Club headquarters in Arcadia Block, then, led by the 4th Infantry Band from Drum Barracks, paraded north through town to the music of "Battle Hymn and various inspiring National airs," to the speakers' stand in front of the Lafayette. Orators of the night's festivities included N. A. Potter, president of the local Union Club, Abel Stearns, John Temple, Manuel Requena, Phineas

[6] *Star*, September 24, 1864.

Banning, and the featured speaker, T. G. Phelps of San Francisco. Afterwards, "all went their way, rejoicing." [7]

A second mammoth Union demonstration reverberated in Los Angeles one week later. Phineas Banning led a Wilmington delegation 200 strong, complete with an eight-horse coach toting the 4th Infantry Band and a huge banner proclaiming "We Are Coming, Father Abraham." As the rally got under way with a procession up Main Street, "guns were fired in quick succession, while the heavens were ablaze with lighted rockets." In front of the Lafayette Hotel, the regular Union gathering place, Banning delivered "a short but most scathing speech against treason and rebellion," followed by a two-hour address by W. E. Lovett of San Francisco. The oratory was so impassioned, according to the *News*, that, "at times, we venture the opinion, there was not a tearless eye in the crowd." [8]

Although the *Star* entered the political war with its usual relish, the newspaper did not finish the campaign. That the journal was having financial troubles was heralded by a notice in the September 3rd issue:

> The undersigned has transferred his interest in the Los Angeles Star to Mr. A. C. Russell, who will hereafter be the Editor and Publisher of this paper, and be alone responsible for any debts contracted.
>
> Parties knowing themselves indebted to the office will please come forward and settle their accounts, and those to whom bills shall be forwarded are expected to make immediate payment thereof.
>
> H. HAMILTON

A. C. Russell, who took over management of the *Star*, was a prominent San Francisco and Sacramento journalist and a Democrat. In mid-September, the paper sent out an agent to collect old debts and receive new subscriptions. The new

[7] *News*, October 18, 1864.
[8] *News*, October 22, 1864.

editor appealed for support from Democrats throughout the southern counties: "Let every man who desires the over-throw of the usurping despot who sits like a hideous demon upon the breast of his country . . . aid in the great work by contributing to the support of Democratic newspapers." But this frantic cry for assistance came too late. The last issue ap-peared on October 1st, a single sheet announcing the sale of the *Star* and the suspension of the paper. Russell, who had assumed control of the newspaper less than a month before, explained that he had only leased the *Star* and that Hamil-ton had reserved the right to sell it. So ended abruptly the only Democratic newspaper in Los Angeles.[9]

Phineas Banning purchased the *Star's* press and materials, paying $1,100 according to the *News*, and moved the paper to Wilmington. The journal now filled its columns with praise for Lincoln and the administration, a turnabout that must have galled Henry Hamilton. After only six issues, to remove the aura of treason associated with the name *Star*, the paper's title was changed to the *Wilmington Journal*. Hamilton left for Arizona in December.[10]

Los Angeles Democrats were chagrined at the suspension of the *Star*, for henceforth their activities in town were re-ported in a far less flattering light by the only journal in town, the Republican-oriented *News*. The newspaper an-nounced a coming Democratic rally with laconic derision: "Everybody who wants to hear the Government abused and the rebels excused should hear the speaking."[11]

In its pre-election issue, the *News* informed voters that they faced a simple black-and-white choice between "divi-sion, dissension and anarchy [McClellan]" or "a firmly united, prosperous, powerful and happy nation [Lincoln]." The same issue carried encouraging reports of Union victories in the East: Grant was hammering Lee before Richmond and

9 *Star*, September 3 and 17, October 1, 1864; Rice, pp. 253–254.
10 *News*, October 1, 11, November 22, 1864; Rice, p. 254.
11 *News*, November 1, 1864.

Petersburg, and Sherman was burning his way through the South.[12]

Election day in Los Angeles passed quietly. The lone disturbance was a rumor, later proved false, that the Stars and Stripes had been ripped down in El Monte.

The initial return indicated a stunning upset. Lincoln was winning nationwide as expected, in California, and—it appeared—in Los Angeles County! There was jubilation among Union men in Los Angeles, and artillery boomed at Drum Barracks. The *News* was in ecstacy that this Democratic bastion had at last fallen to the Union: "We have met the enemy and they are ours. Los Angeles County has atoned in part for its former political sins by repudiating the bogus Democracy. ... We have come, Father Abraham!"[13]

The Los Angeles County returns revealed monumental disparities among some of the precincts:

	Lincoln	*McClellan*
Los Angeles (city)	299	341
El Monte	18	144
Wilmington	312	2
Drum Barracks	187	0

In the county as a whole, the returns showed Lincoln with 872 votes and McClellan with 593, giving the former a majority of 279 in a region that had never before voted against the Democratic Party.[14]

A week later, Union men held a joyous demonstration in Los Angeles. A twelve-pounder was hauled from Drum Barracks and dragged to the top of the hill behind the Plaza, where the cumbersome weapon promptly fired a 100-gun salute. After a torchlight procession around town, Union supporters gathered around the Lafayette Hotel to hear Col-

[12] *Ibid.*, November 5, 1864.
[13] *Ibid.*, November 1, 1864.
[14] *News*, November 12, 1864; *Daily Alta California*, November 10, 19, 1864.

onel Curtis give a rousing victory speech. "A conspicuous feature of the celebration," wrote the Los Angeles correspondent of the *Alta California*, "was the illumination of W. W. Buffum's store and saloon. Mr. Buffum, a whole souled Union man, as generous as he is patriotic, had given notice that the proceeds of his sales during the day and evening would be donated to the Sanitary Fund. . . . The United States Hotel was also illuminated, and from the roof of the Court House a fine display of fire-works were set off as the procession marched past."[15]

But the Union jubilation in Los Angeles County was premature and, as it turned out, in error. On November 17th, the County Board of Canvassers created anger and disgust among Lincoln supporters by throwing out the returns from four precincts: Wilmington, San José [Pomona], Azusa, and Fort Tejon. 474 votes were rejected, most of them Union, giving McClellan Los Angeles County by a majority of 191. The reason for voiding the ballots in the four precincts, according to the Board, was that the returns from these precincts showed irregularities and were not properly signed by precinct officials. Unionists gave a different reason: county officials were "intensely McClellan or Secessionists." The *News* complained that "Nearly one quarter of the voters of the county have been disfranchised." Wilmington voters threatened legal action against the Board of Supervisors, but apparently never pursued the matter. The decision of the county Board was allowed to stand, and Los Angeles County once again stood in the Democratic column.[16]

Dissatisfaction with the County Board of Supervisors extended beyond election irregularities. William Buffum and John Jones, two Los Angeles merchants loyal to the Union, charged that their tax assessments, and those of others who

[15] *Daily Alta California*, November 23, 1864. The San Francisco paper printed a "Letter from Los Angeles," written by one who signed himself "Viejo," every six to eight days.
[16] *News*, November 19, 1864; *Alta California*, November 23, December 6, 1864.

expressed Union sentiments, had been raised by the Board as much as $1,000. They further claimed that the Board of Supervisors, along with many civic and business leaders in Los Angeles, "have, with but few and marked exceptions . . . manifested a bitter and determined hostility to the American Government." [17]

As the year 1864 drew to a close, even the most dyed-in-the-wool secessionist could see that victory would soon come for the Union. The Confederacy was shrinking almost daily as Grant held Lee in a steel vise before Richmond, and Sherman was running wild through Georgia and South Carolina. Rumors began to circulate locally that a number of Los Angeles secessionists were planning to emigrate to Mexico. The plan, according to the *Alta*'s Los Angeles correspondent, was for a large group of local citizens to establish a colony in Baja California, then offer their allegiance to Emperor Maximilian. Baja California would then become a haven for Confederates who "wish to free themselves from the despotism of Lincoln." To plan this emigration, said the *Alta*'s correspondent, "meetings of the Knights are said to be more frequent." This was an apparent reference to the Knights of the Golden Circle, the secret pro-Confederate organization said to be active in southern California. Interestingly, this is one of the very rare mentions of the secret organization in the contemporary press.[18] Needless to say, nothing ever came of the Baja California colonization scheme.

[17] *Alta California,* November 23, 1864.
[18] *Ibid.,* December 22, 1864.

General Phineas Banning, standing,
with Matthew Keller, left, and John B. Hollister, right

TRIUMPH AND TRAGEDY

WINTER RAINS almost annually turned the Los Angeles–San Pedro road into a quagmire. If the precipitation was unusually heavy, freight transportation between the harbor and Los Angeles came to a halt, and the city's commerce was adversely affected. The ideal solution, many thought, was a railroad. But railroads were expensive, and capital to build them was hard to come by in southern California in the mid-1860s. The dream of a Los Angeles–San Pedro railroad had been simmering for a number of years. In 1861, Los Angeles assemblymen Abel Stearns and Murray Morrison were able to persuade the state legislature to grant a franchise for such a purpose. But the war and other pressing matters intervened, and the franchise was allowed to die.[1]

In December 1864, the railroad plan was again broached. Businessmen from Los Angeles, Wilmington, and San Pedro met for several days in the County Court House to mull over the prospect of a harbor railroad to satisfy commercial needs. A proposal was aired to construct the road from Los Angeles to Wilmington, then on out to Deadman's Island, where a wharf and breakwater would be built. To finance the railroad, Los Angeles County was asked to subscribe $100,000, the city $50,000, and the balance would be raised by private investment. "There can be no doubt," the *Alta's* correspon-

[1] Newmark, pp. 295–296.

dent wrote, "but that the business now carried on over the road from this city [Los Angeles] to San Pedro and Wilmington would pay a handsome dividend on the capital requisite to build and equip the road." But again the project was allowed to languish, and it was not until 1869 that the Los Angeles–San Pedro Railroad, the first in southern California, would become a reality.[2]

Another commercial venture—one that promised large rewards in the future—was begun in Los Angeles in January 1865. The Pioneer Oil Company was organized with Phineas Banning as president and John G. Downey as secretary. Others who invested in the project to recover petroleum from a field three miles west of town included Benjamin D. Wilson, John S. Griffin, Mathew Keller, and Charles Ducommun. "It will be no small astonishment to our citizens," wrote the *News*, "to find that incalculable fortunes lie in the very substance with which, as many of them believe, they have been sorely afflicted, that which they have scraped from their shoes for three-quarters of a century past." A steam engine and boring machinery arrived in Wilmington in February, and were immediately hauled to the new oil field. By early summer, petroleum and "coal oil," or kerosene, from the Brea field and Pico Spring were being refined and sold in Los Angeles at a cost of ten cents a gallon.[3]

A boon to Wilmington and nearby Drum Barracks was the completion, early in 1865, of the great water ditch from the San Gabriel River. The seven-mile long project was initiated in April 1864 by 200 soldiers from Drum Barracks. They worked without pay other than their miniscule soldiers' wages, preferring this to drab camp duties. A dam was built on the river high enough to divert water into the long ditch. Banning furnished 100,000 feet of lumber for fluming the ditch, and supervised construction. Farming was now possible

[2] *Alta California*, December 10, 1864; *News*, December 3, 1864; Newmark, p. 334.
[3] *News*, January 31, February 4, 11, 18, 1865; Newmark, p. 346.

in the drought-ridden lands around the port town and army post.[4]

To help alleviate the suffering of Union soldiers wounded in battle, the Sanitary Commission had long been active in California. San Francisco had provided the lion's share of the state's contributions to the Sanitary fund, while southern California, much to the disgust of Banning and other local loyalists, had collected next to nothing. With the view of stimulating donations from this part of the state, a group of Los Angeles citizens assembled in Temple Block on January 5, 1865 to organize a Soldiers' Aid Society. Joseph B. Mallard, justice of the peace and former county coroner, was elected chairman of the organization, and active efforts were begun to secure new members and subscriptions. Next month, chapters of the Soldiers Aid Society were formed in Wilmington, San Pedro, El Monte, San Bernardino, and San Diego. A door-to-door canvas was initiated, and, at last, respectable sums were collected. Wilmington, led by the indominable Banning, led all southern California chapters in the amount of money subscribed. By month's end, Los Angeles County had contributed $1,170 in greenbacks and $139 in coin.[5]

Perhaps a major contributing factor to the new-found generosity of Los Angeles citizens was the news of the glorious Union victories in the East. The fall of Savannah became known in Los Angeles early in January, and the capture of Charleston, South Carolina, birthplace of the rebel effort, was announced in the *News* the following month. Both victories set off spontaneous demonstrations among the Union faithful in Los Angeles, and the booming of cannon in Wilmington. Rumors of Confederate peace commissioners seeking an armistice on Union terms sent loyal spirits even higher. The war appeared to be nearing its conclusion.

---

[4] *News*, January 21, 1865; Hunt, *Army of the Pacific*, p. 44. It should be noted that, in 1865, the San Gabriel River joined the Los Angeles and flowed as one into the harbor. Below the junction of the two streams, the river now known as the Los Angeles bore the name of San Gabriel.

[5] *News*, January 3 and 7, February 4, 1865.

The *News* expressed fear that the defeated Confederate army might seek refuge in southern California: "The broken fragments of the rebel army must have some hiding place. . . . It would not be astonishing if this portion of California, and Arizona, were overrun with score upon scores of rebels, fresh from the battlefields of the Potomac, within the next eight months." The newspaper complained that the military authorities in California were not taking the threat seriously.[6]

Lincoln's second inaugural address was received without much enthusiasm by the *News*. "That the Inaugural means something it is likely," stated the editor, "but that something cannot be arrived at by reading the same." The president's "Malice toward none, with charity to all" sentiments seemed too conciliatory to the *News*; the rebels had committed treason and killed thousands of American boys, and they should be justly punished for their crimes.[7]

The glorious news for which Union men had waited patiently four years—the fall of the Confederate capital of Richmond—arrived by telegraph from San Francisco on the morning of April 4th. Immediately citizens poured into the streets, shouting and dancing. In Buffums' Saloon, toasts were joyously offered to General Grant and "Old Abe."[8]

Six days later—at 10 a.m., April 10th—the telegraph flashed a bulletin to Los Angeles announcing Lee's surrender. "A simultaneous firing of guns sprang up in all parts of the city, which, with a general merriment among Union citizens, was continued all night," reported the *News*. The newspaper appeared next day with banner columns: "GLORIOUS NEWS! SURRENDER OF GEN. LEE! AND HIS ENTIRE ARMY! Hang out your banners—Let patriots rejoice to the full—the rebellion is crushed."[9]

[6] *News*, March 7, 1865.
[7] *News*, March 14, 1865.
[8] *News*, April 8, 1865.
[9] *News*, April 11, 1865.

Wilmington and Drum Barracks did not learn of the surrender until the morning of April 11th, when Colonel Curtis received the following telegraphed dispatch from the governor:

Sacramento, April 10, 1865

To Colonel James E. Curtis
   Drum Barracks
Lee, with his whole army, has surrendered to Grant.

F. F. Low, Governor

As dawn broke over Drum Barracks, cannons erupted in flame, and the booming continued most of the morning. In Wilmington, bells added to the antiphony of sound. In the afternoon, the infantry paraded through town, followed by the Native California Cavalry under Captain de la Guerra of Santa Barbara, just returned from border duty, resplendent on their beautiful mounts and flourishing swords. The celebration lasted far into the night.[10]

Saturday morning, April 15th, 1865, dawned like any other day in Los Angeles. The victory celebrations were over, and the town was returning to normal. At 9:20 a.m., the telegraph began clicking in the little telegraph office in Temple Block. The operator began routinely taking down the message. Before he was half through, his face turned ashen. He hurriedly completed transcribing the dispatch and, hands shaking, gave it to the office manager. The short message from San Francisco read as follows:

PRESIDENT LINCOLN AND SECRETARY SEWARD WERE ASSASSINATED IN WASHINGTON LAST NIGHT. THE PRESIDENT DIED THIS MORNING; SEWARD STILL ALIVE BUT NOT EXPECTED TO LIVE.

The awful news struck like a thunderbolt from a cloudless sky. It spread throughout town like a prairie fire. Men were

[10] Krythe, *Port Admiral*, p. 136.

running pell mell through the streets, shouting the calami-
tous tidings; others wept openly or stood frozen in immobi-
lity, too stunned to comprehend. A crowd quickly gathered
at the telegraph office, awaiting further dispatches. Perhaps,
some thought. it was a cruel hoax.

At 11:00 a.m., a second message arrived over the wire,
confirming the national tragedy:

DEATH OF PRESIDENT LINCOLN IS CONFIRMED;
SEWARD STILL ALIVE.

One more dispatch reached Los Angeles a short while later.
giving some details of the assassination and naming Booth
as the murderer. Then the lines went dead. The *News* reported that the military authorities, fearing some revolutionary plot, closed down the telegraph in California for a
48-hour period.[11]

The remainder of the day was a nightmare of grief, confusion, and, on the part of some former secessionists in town,
elation. Dr. John S. Griffin was visiting Harris Newmark
when the news reached them of the president's death. Newmark described the scene: "While we were seated together
by an open window in the dining room, a man named Kane
ran by on the street, shouting out the momentous news that
Abraham Lincoln had been shot! Griffin, who was a staunch
Southerner, was on his feet instantly, cheering for Jeff Davis.
He gave evidence, indeed, of great mental excitement, and
soon seized his hat and rushed for the door, hurrahing for
the Confederacy. In a flash, I realized that Griffin would be
in awful jeopardy if he reached the street in that unbalanced
condition, and by main force I held him back, convincing
him at last of his folly. In later years the genial Doctor

---

11 *News*, April 18, 1865. This issue of the paper had black borders around all
of its news columns. This writer was unable to verify the *News'* story that the
telegraph lines were closed down to head off a revolutionary plot.

frankly admitted that I had undoubtedly saved him from certain death."[12]

The news of Lincoln's assassination came as a profound shock to Los Angeles, and for several days a pall of sorrow hung heavy over the city. Although a number of Southern sympathizers, on first impulse, expressed exultation, on deeper thought most of them realized the tragic consequences of the act to the nation and quickly suppressed any display of joy.[13]

On April 17th the telegraph lines reopened, and a dispatch reached Los Angeles announcing that Lincoln's funeral would take place on the 19th at 12 noon. The city's common council, after passing appropriate resolutions of sympathy and denunciations of the "murderous act," declared April 19th a day of mourning.

From Department of the Pacific headquarters in San Francisco, an order reached Colonel Curtis at Drum Barracks to promptly arrest anyone "so utterly infamous as to exult over the assassination of the President." The News added that several former secessionists in Los Angeles were "a fit subject for the hangman," having been overheard making distastful remarks regarding the martyred President. Soldiers from Drum Barracks established themselves in town and, within two days, arrested six men—including "Nigger Pete" Biggs —for allegedly glorifying the murder of Lincoln. All but "Nigger Pete" were released soon afterwards, prompting the News to condemn Colonel Curtis for leniency toward treason.[14]

On April 19th all stores were closed and business suspended. Shortly before 12 noon, silent crowds assembled in front of Arcadia Block for the funeral procession. Present was a company of dismounted cavalry from Drum Barracks, a large delegation of federal, state, and county officials, the

12 Newmark, p. 337.
13 Ibid., p. 338.
14 News, April 22 and 25, 1865.

mayor and common council, various lodges and societies, the Union League, and scores of private citizens. Promptly at noon, to the sound of funeral music and muffled drums, the procession moved slowly west on Arcadia Street to Main, down Main Street to Spring as far as First, east of First Street to Main, and up Main to the City Hall. A funeral oration was preached by the Reverend Elias Birdsall, Episcopal clergyman, in the upper floor of the County Court House. The sermon "drew tears from eyes all unused to weep." Afterwards, prayers were offered for the martyred president and the bereaved nation. In all, it was a solemn day in the history of Los Angeles.[15]

A month later, the city election resulted in a Unionist victory, the first such happening in Los Angeles of the Civil War period. José Mascarel was elected mayor, and the entire Union ticket won office in a city that had always before been strongly secessionist-minded. The triumph of the North and the shock of Lincoln's assassination were apparently enough to alter the political complexion of Los Angeles.[16]

[15] *News*, April 22, 1865; Newmark, pp. 338–339.
[16] *News*, May 2, 1865; Newmark, p. 339.

EPILOGUE

WAR'S BITTER AFTERTASTE lingered on in Los Angeles for several years. Former secessionists and Union men were not on speaking terms, and, according to Harris Newmark, "it was some time before noticeable progress was felt here."[1] Major Horace Bell, upon returning in 1866 from war service in the Union Army, complained that his reception in Los Angeles was distinctly hostile: "Old friends, with a few honorable exceptions such as Judge A. J. King and Col. E. J. C. Kewen, turned their backs on me. 'The idea,' said they, 'of a Los Angeles man of your stamp fighting on the side of the blacks!'" Bell referred to himself as "a red flag to the Secessionist bulls of the vicinity," particularly in El Monte, where he was allegedly attacked on several occasions. Another Union veteran, Charles Jenkins, fresh from Andersonville Prison, was greeted in Los Angeles with so little acclaim that he temporarily removed himself to Santa Catalina.[2]

Returning Confederate veterans also found the going rough at first. Captain Cameron E. Thom landed in San Pedro penniless; John Griffin advanced him money enough to reach Los Angeles and begin life anew. Brigadier General J. Lan-

[1] Newmark, p. 339.
[2] Bell, pp. 76–81. Bell also wrote, perhaps with literary exaggeration of which he was justly famous, "Los Angeles at the close of the Rebellion was the most vindictive, uncompromising community in the United States."

[163]

caster Brent, former Los Angeles attorney, never came back, but settled in New Orleans instead.[3]

But time is a great healer, and by the end of the 1860s the bitterness had mellowed considerably. The enmity between Phineas Banning, a staunch Unionist during the war, and John S. Griffin, rabid Southerner, disappeared completely. Both men worked closely together to develop the Los Angeles and San Pedro Railroad in 1869, and were later allied in a number of other business ventures. When Griffin died, he was eulogized by none other than Henry D. Barrows, former United States Marshal in Los Angeles who, during the war years, had attempted to jail all secessionists, Griffin included.[4]

The major symbol of the Civil War, as far as Los Angeles was concerned, was Drum Barracks. With the conflict over, there was no longer need for the army to maintain such a large supply depot. Hence, the army abandoned Drum Barracks in 1866, causing a great deal of economic discomfort in Wilmington. In 1873 the camp was offered by the government at public auction, and was purchased for under $10,000 by Benjamin D. Wilson, one of the original owners. The buildings of Drum Barracks, erected at so much expense in 1862–1864, were either sold at auction and removed, destroyed by fire, or, in the case of the officers' quarters, allowed to remain intact on the premises. Today, the Wilmington site of Drum Barracks officers' quarters is recognized as a California Historical Landmark—the only tangible remembrance left of the Civil War period in Los Angeles.[5]

Henry Hamilton returned to Los Angeles in 1868 and resumed publication of the *Los Angeles Star*, the "late unpleasantness," as he termed it, behind him. No longer a burning partisan, Hamilton molded the new *Star* into a respectable journal, a "model" newspaper according to Los Angeles his-

[3] Newmark, pp. 339–340.
[4] Krythe, *Port Admiral*, pp. 166–175; H. D. Barrows, "Memorial Sketch of Dr. John S. Griffin," *H.S.S.C. Annual Publications*, 1898.
[5] Newmark, p. 358; Society for the Preservation of Drum Barracks, p. 3.

torian J. M. Guinn. Hamilton edited the *Star* for four years, then leased it for a year, resumed his editorship, and finally leased it again, in 1873, to Ben C. Truman, author of several books promoting southern California. The colorful Truman guided the newspaper until 1877, giving way to a succession of mediocre editors who tried their hand until 1879. In that year, the *Star* ceased publication for good when the sheriff attached its materials.[6]

Great change came to Los Angeles during the two decades following the Civil War. The arrival of the Southern Pacific Railroad in 1876 and the great boom of the 80s brought commercial importance and population growth to the city, turning it into the leading metropolis of the south and a worthy rival to San Francisco. The Civil War interlude faded into a colorful and rather unpleasant memory of an era past.

[6] J. M. Guinn, "La Estrella: The Pioneer Newspaper of Los Angeles," *H.S. S.C. Annual Publication,* 1900; Rice, pp. 259–260.

BIBLIOGRAPHY

BIBLIOGRAPHY

OFFICIAL RECORDS

The War of the Rebellion: A Compilation of the Official Records of the Union and Confederate Armies (Washington, D.C., 1880–1901). Series I, Volume L, Parts 1 and 2.

BOOKS AND PAMPHLETS

Bancroft, Hubert Howe, *History of California*, Vol. VII (San Francisco: The History Co., 1890).

Beattie, George William and Helen Pruitt Beattie, *Heritage of the Valley: San Bernardino's First Century* (Oakland: Biobooks, 1951).

Bell, Horace, *Reminiscences of a Ranger* (Santa Barbara: Wallace Hebbard, 1927).

Bell, Horace, *On the Old West Coast: Being Further Reminiscences of a Ranger*, ed. by Lanier Bartlett (New York: Grosset and Dunlap, 1930).

Bowman, Lynn, *Los Angeles: Epic of a City* (Berkeley: Howell–North Books, 1974).

Buchanan, Russell, *David S. Terry of California: Dueling Judge* (San Marino: The Huntington Library, 1956).

Clark, George T., *Leland Stanford: War Governor of California, Railroad Builder and Founder of Stanford University* (Stanford: Stanford University Press, 1931).

Cleland, Robert Glass, *From Wilderness to Empire: A History of California, 1542–1900* (New York: Alfred A. Knopf, 1944).

Cleland, Robert Glass, *The Cattle on a Thousand Hills* (San Marino: The Huntington Library, 1964).

[169]

Colton, Ray C., *The Civil War in the Western Territories* (Norman: University of Oklahoma Press, 1959).

Davidson, Homer K., *Black Jack Davidson: A Cavalry Commander on the Western Frontier* (Glendale: Arthur H. Clark Co., 1974).

Davis, Winfield J., *History of Political Conventions in California, 1849– 1892* (Sacramento: California State Library, 1893).

Doran, Adelaide LeMert, *The Ranch That Was Robbins': Santa Catalina Island, California* (Los Angeles: privately printed, 1964).

Ellison, Joseph, *California and the Nation, 1850–1869* (Berkeley: University of California Press, 1927).

Giffen, Helen S. and Arthur Woodward, *The Story of El Tejon* (Los Angeles: Dawson's Book Shop, 1942).

Hancock, Almira, *Reminiscences of Winfield Scott Hancock by His Wife* (New York: Charles L. Webster & Co., 1887).

Hayes, Judge Benjamin, *Pioneer Notes from the Diaries of Judge Benjamin Hayes, 1849–1875*, ed. by Marjorie T. Wolcott (Los Angeles: privately printed, 1929).

Hunt, Aurora, *The Army of the Pacific, 1860–1866* (Glendale: Arthur H. Clark Co., 1951).

Hunt, Aurora, *Major General James Henry Carleton, 1814–1873, Western Frontier Dragoon* (Glendale: Arthur H. Clark Co., 1958).

Hunt, Rockwell D. and Nellie Van de Grift Sanchez, *A Short History of California* (New York: Thomas Y. Crowell Co., 1929).

Johnston, William Preston, *The Life of General Albert Sidney Johnston* (New York: D. Appleton & Co., 1878).

Kennedy, Elijah R., *The Contest for California in 1861* (Boston: Houghton Mifflin Co., 1912).

Kibby, Leo P., *California, The Civil War, and the Indian Problem* (Los Angeles: Lorrin L. Morrison, 1967).

Krythe, Maymie, *Port Admiral: Phineas Banning, 1830–1885* (San Francisco: California Historical Society, 1957).

Layne, J. Gregg, *Annals of Los Angeles* (San Francisco: California Historical Society, 1935).

Lewis, Oscar, *The War in the Far West, 1861–1865* (Garden City: Doubleday & Co., 1961).

Moore, Avery C., *Destiny's Soldier* (San Francisco: Fearon Publishers, 1958).

Morrison, Lorrin L., *Warner: The Man and the Ranch* (Los Angeles: published by the author, 1962).

Nadeau, Remi, *Los Angeles: From Mission to Modern City* (New York: Longman's Green and Co., 1960).

Newmark, Harris, *Sixty Years in Southern California*, ed. by Maurice H. and Marco R. Newmark, 4th edition ed. by W. W. Robinson (Los Angeles: Zeitlin & Ver Brugge, 1970).

Pitt, Leonard, *The Decline of the Californios: A Social History of the Spanish-Speaking Californios, 1846–1890* (Berkeley: University of California Press, 1970).

Rice, William B., *The Los Angeles Star, 1851–1864: The Beginnings of Journalism in Southern California* (Berkeley: University of California Press, 1947).

Robinson, William W., *The Island of Santa Catalina* (Los Angeles: Title Guarantee and Trust Co., 1941).

Robinson, William W., *The Indians of Los Angeles: Story of the Liquidation of a People* (Los Angeles: Glen Dawson, 1952).

Robinson, William W., *Lawyers of Los Angeles* (Los Angeles: Los Angeles Bar Association, 1959).

Roland, Charles P., *Albert Sidney Johnston: Soldier of Three Republics* (Austin: University of Texas Press, 1964).

Scherer, James A. B., *Thirty-first Star* (New York: G. P. Putnam's Sons, 1942).

Society for the Preservation of Drum Barracks, *Drum Barracks and the Camel Corps* (Wilmington, 1965).

Spalding, William A., *History and Reminiscences: Los Angeles City and County, California* (Los Angeles: J. R. Finnell & Sons, 1931).

Tucker, Glenn, *Hancock The Superb* (Indianapolis: Bobbs-Merrill Co., 1960).

Wagoner, Jay J., *Early Arizona: Prehistory to Civil War* (Tucson: University of Arizona Press, 1975).

Willard, Charles Dwight, *The Herald's History of Los Angeles* (Los Angeles: Kingsley-Barnes & Neuner Co., 1901).

Wilson, J. Albert, *History of Los Angeles County, California*, reproduction (Berkeley: Howell–North, 1959).

PERIODICAL ARTICLES

Barrows, Henry D., "Memorial Sketch of Dr. John S. Griffin," *H.S.S.C. Annual Publication*, 1898.

Blew, Robert W., "Vigilantism in Los Angeles, 1835–1874," *Southern California Quarterly*, Spring 1972.

Carson, James F., "California: Gold to Help Finance the War," *Journal of the West*, January 1975.

Caughey, John Walton, "Don Benito Wilson: An Average Southern Californian," *Huntington Library Quarterly*, April 1939.

Clendenen, Clarence C., "Dan Showalter—California Secessionist," *C.H.S. Quarterly*, December 1961.

Clendenen, Clarence C., "A Confederate Spy in California," *Southern California Quarterly*, September 1963.

Colburn, E. C., "Swank Drum Barracks—It Saved the Union," *Westways*, March 1942.

Cooney, Percival, "Southern California in Civil War Days," *Annual Publication, H.S.S.C.*, 1924.

Dustin, Charles Mial, "The Knights of the Golden Circle," *Pacific Monthly*, November 1911.

Giffin, Helen S., "Camp Independence—An Owens Valley Outpost," *H.S. S.C. Quarterly*, December 1942.

Gilbert, Benjamin Franklin, "The Confederate Minority in California," *C.H.S. Quarterly*, June 1941.

Gilbert, Benjamin Franklin, "The Mythical Johnston Conspiracy," *C.H.S. Quarterly*, June 1949.

Gilbert, Benjamin Franklin, "California and the Civil War: A Bibliographical Essay," *C.H.S. Quarterly*, December 1961.

Goldman, Harry H., "Southern Sympathy in Southern California, 1860–1865," *Journal of the West*, October 1965.

Guinn, James M., "La Estrella: The Pioneer Newspaper of Los Angeles," *H.S.S.C. Annual Publication*, 1900.

Guinn, James M., "The Lost Mines of Santa Catalina," *Annual Publications, H.S.S.C.*, 1912–1913.

Hunsaker, William J., "Lansford W. Hastings' Project for the Invasion and Conquest of Arizona and New Mexico for the Southern Confederacy," *Arizona Historical Review*, July 1931.

Hyman, Harold M., "New Light on Cohen v. Wright: California's First Loyalty Oath Case," *P.H.R.*, May 1959.

King, William F., "El Monte, An American Town in Southern California, 1851–1866," *Southern California Quarterly*, December 1971.

Kornweibel, Theodore, Jr., "The Occupation of Santa Catalina Island During the Civil War," *C.H.S. Quarterly*, December 1967.

Krythe, Maymie R., "First Hotel in Old Los Angeles, The Romantic Bella Union," *H.S.S.C. Quarterly*, June 1951.

Newmark, Marco R., "Medical Profession in the Early Days of Los Angeles," *H.S.S.C. Quarterly*, March 1952.

Scammell, J. M., "Military Units in Southern California, 1853–1862," *C.H.S. Quarterly*, September 1950.

Spaulding, Imogene, "The Attitude of California to the Civil War," *Annual Publications, H.S.S.C.*, 1912–1913.

Waitman, Leonard B., "The Knights of the Golden Circle," *San Bernardino County Museum Association Quarterly*, Summer 1968.

Walters, Helen B., "Confederates in Southern California," *H.S.S.C. Quarterly*, March 1953.

Wang, Peter Heywood, "The Mythical Confederate Plot in Southern California," *San Bernardino County Museum Association Quarterly*, Summer 1969.

Watford, W. H., "The Far-Western Wing of the Rebellion, 1861–1865," *C.H.S. Quarterly*, June 1955.

Weight, Harold and Lucille, "Forgotten Road to Gold," *Westerners Brand Book*, Book Ten, Los Angeles Corral, Westerners, 1963.

Woodward, Art, "Confederate Secret Societies in California," *Westerners Brand Book*, Los Angeles Corral, Westerners, 1949.

NEWSPAPERS

Daily Alta California (San Francisco), 1864–1865

Los Angeles Semi-Weekly Southern News, 1860–1865 (name changed to *Los Angeles Tri-Weekly News* 1864–1865)

Los Angeles Star, 1856–1864

San Francisco Bulletin, 1861–1862

Southern Vineyard (Los Angeles), 1859

For Further Reading

Additional Works Published through 2012

Los Angeles in Civil War Days was published by Dawson's Book Shop of Los Angeles some three decades ago in a limited edition of three hundred copies. That first edition, reprinted here in paperback for the first time, is now exceedingly hard to find. It remains the only published book-length study of Los Angeles during this time of national crisis. The volume stands on its own, with only a few minor revisions. What is identified as Butterfield's Overland Stage Line was actually the Overland Mail Company (p. 24). Sergeant William McCleave of Company K, 1st U.S. Dragoons, not Lieutenant Beale, escorted the 31 camels from Fort Tejon to Los Angeles, reaching the latter on or about June 19, 1861. The army's attempt to form a Camel Corps was unsuccessful (pp. 59, 94). Alonzo Ridley was deputy sheriff of Los Angeles County when he led his small group to the Confederacy (p. 62).

For the reader who desires to learn more about Los Angeles, and California in general, during the Civil War era, listed below are a number of more recent studies that shed light on the subject.

An excellent unpublished study needs to be mentioned. Albert Lewis's "Los Angeles in the Civil War Decades, 1850–

1868" (Ph.D. dissertation, University of Southern California, 1970) uses a number of manuscript sources to reveal the thoughts, motives, and plans of several Civil War–era Los Angeles citizens.

Although no other general studies of Los Angeles in the 1860s have yet appeared, a number of biographies have been published in recent years that shed light on several of the town's leaders during the Civil War.

There was no more fervent supporter of the Union cause in Southern California than Phineas Banning. Tom Sitton's *Grand Ventures: The Banning Family and the Shaping of Southern California* (San Marino, California, 2010) details the life and adventures of Phineas Banning and his family. An enigma in Los Angeles was Benjamin Wilson; he was a strong Southern Democrat, but with Banning, he donated the land in Wilmington for Drum Barracks, the main Union Army center in Southern California during the Civil War period. Nat B. Read's *Don Benito Wilson, Los Angeles, 1841–1878* (Santa Monica, 2008) recounts his life, particularly his years in the Los Angeles area. The only Army officer in Los Angeles at the outset of the war was Captain Winfield Scott Hancock. David M. Jordan's *Winfield Scott Hancock: A Soldier's Life* (Indianapolis, 1988) well covers his short Los Angeles experiences in the chapter "In California." My own article "A California Copperhead: Henry Hamilton and the Los Angeles Star," *Arizona and the West* (Autumn 1981), explores the life and experiences of the strongly pro-Southern editor of the *Los Angeles Star* newspaper. Another outspoken Confederate sympathizer was Edward J. C. Kewen; his stormy life is explored in this writer's "Colonel E. J. C. Kewen: Los Angeles Fire Eating Orator of the Civil War Era," *Southern California Quarterly* (Summer 1979). A fine study of the Democratic Party's dilemma at the time is Ronald Woolsey, "The Politics of a Lost Cause: 'Seceshers' and Democrats in Southern California during the Civil War," *California History* (Winter 1990–91).

Today, the old officers' quarters at Drum Barracks in Wilmington is the sole tangible memento of the Civil War period in Los Angeles. Don McDowell's *The Beat of the Drum: The History, Events and People of Drum Barracks* (Wilmington, California, Drum Barracks, 1993) covers the story of this important military post. Don Chaput's "The Civil War Military Outpost on Catalina Island," *Southern California Quarterly* (Spring 1993), tells the history of this off-shore bastion during the time of crisis. Myths and half-truths surround the short-lived epic of the U.S. Army's proposed camel corps. The strange beasts of burden left Fort Tejon and briefly were corralled in Los Angeles, then at the Army's Quartermaster Depot in Wilmington, before being herded north to Benecia to be auctioned off. George Stammerjohan's "The U.S. Government Camel Experience," *California Historian* (March 1994), sets the record straight on this unique experiment.

Los Angeles in the Civil War years can be better understood within the context of California and southwestern history. Sentiments were deeply divided between pro-Union and pro-Confederacy sympathizers; Northern California leaned toward the Union, while the southern part of the state, made up of many recent arrivals from the slave states, generally favored the Southern cause. A superb study of pre-war California and local events leading up to the conflict is Leonard Richards's *The California Gold Rush and the Coming of the Civil War* (New York, 2007). Judson Grenier's "Colonel Jack Watson: Copperhead Assemblyman in Civil War California," *Californians* (July 1995), explores the tribulations of a secesh-minded member of the California legislature.

The premier historian of Civil War California is Robert Chandler, recently retired as historian for Wells Fargo, San Francisco. Chandler's "The Press and Civil Liberties in California during the Civil War, 1861–1865" (Ph.D. dissertation,

University of California, Riverside, 1978) was his first scholarly work on the subject. Since then, among his multiple writ-
ings have appeared "California during the Civil War," *Dogtown
Territorial Quarterly* (Fall 1997); "The Velvet Glove: The Army
during the Secession Crisis in California, 1860–1861," *Journal of
the West* (October 1981); "Crushing Dissent: The Pacific Coast
Tests Lincoln's Policy of Suppression," *Civil War History* (September 1984); "Censoring Civil War Journalism in California,"
California Territorial Quarterly (Fall 2002); "An Uncertain Influence: The Role of the Federal Government in California, 1846–
1880," in *Taming the Elephant: Politics, Government, and Law in
Pioneer California* (Berkeley, 2003).

In 1861 Major Sherod Hunter led a Confederate force
from Texas into Arizona Territory, capturing Tucson, with one
small detachment reaching within eighty miles of the Colorado
River. Exaggerated fears of a Confederate invasion gripped Los
Angeles Unionists. The episode is covered in L. Boyd Finch's
*Confederate Pathway to the Pacific: Major Sherod Hunter and Arizona
Territory, CSA* (Tucson, 1996). Later, California Volunteers, who
took over from the Regular Army, marched into Arizona Territory, retook Tucson, and performed garrison duty there until
war's end. See Andrew E. Masich, *The Civil War in Arizona* (Norman, Okla., 2006).

The references described above can enrich the reader's
understanding of Civil War Los Angeles and the Far Southwest. They offer a wealth of supplementary context to the story
offered in *Los Angeles in Civil War Days*.

Fullerton, California
September 1, 2011

Illustration Credits

Bancroft Library, University of California, Berkeley: 44, 53
California Historical Society: 44, 53, 60
Laurence G. Jones: 128 (map)
Huntington Library, San Marino, Calif.: 22, 23, 26, 27, 41, 40 (all),
    56, 57, 60, 97 (top), 100
Title Insurance and Trust Company: 44, 97, 154

INDEX

www.ingramcontent.com/pod-product-compliance
Lightning Source LLC
Chambersburg PA
CBHW021402090426
42742CB00009B/968